easy to make!
Family Meals in Minutes

Good Housekeeping

easy to make!
Family Meals
in Minutes

COLLINS & BROWN

This edition published in Great Britain in 2011
by Collins & Brown
10 Southcombe Street
London W14 0RA

An imprint of Anova Books Company Ltd

First published in Great Britain in 2009

The Good Housekeeping website is
www.allaboutyou.com/goodhousekeeping

10 9 8 7 6 5 4 3 2 1

ISBN 978-1-84340-655-6

A catalogue record for this book is available from the British
Library.

Reproduction by Dot Gradations Ltd
Printed and bound by Times Offset, Malaysia

This book can be ordered direct from the publisher at
www.anovabooks.com

Contents

Foreword

Cooking, for me, is one of life's great pleasures. Not only is it necessary to fuel your body, but it exercises creativity, skill, social bonding and patience. The science behind the cooking also fascinates me, learning to understand how yeast works, or to grasp why certain flavours marry quite so well (in my mind) is to become a good cook.

I've often encountered people who claim not to be able to cook – they're just not interested or say they simply don't have time. My sister won't mind me saying that she was one of those who sat firmly in the camp of disinterested domestic goddess. But things change, she realised that my mother (an excellent cook) can't always be on hand to prepare steaming home-cooked meals and that she actually wanted to become a mother one day who was able to whip up good food for her own family. All it took was some good cook books (naturally, Good Housekeeping was present and accounted for) and some enthusiasm and sure enough she is now a kitchen wizard, creating such confections that even baffle me.

I've been lucky enough to have had a love for all things culinary since as long as I can remember. Baking rock-like chocolate cakes and misshapen biscuits was a right of passage that I protectively guard. I made my mistakes young, so have lost the fear of cookery mishaps. I think it's these mishaps that scare people, but when you realise that a mistake made once will seldom be repeated, then kitchen domination can start.

This Good Housekeeping Easy to Make! collection is filled with hundreds of tantalising recipes that have been triple tested (at least!) in our dedicated test kitchens. They have been developed to be easily achievable, delicious and guaranteed to work – taking the chance out of cooking.

I hope you enjoy this collection and that it inspires you to get cooking.

Meike.

Meike Beck
Cookery Editor
Good Housekeeping

0

The Basics

Planning Midweek Meals

It can be quite a challenge to make sure that every member of the family eats healthy and balanced meals, especially if they come home at different times after various activities. If you plan each week's menu in advance, it will take the stress out of deciding what to cook each day and you can turn leftovers into meals in their own right.

Different types of midweek meals

Midweek meals are not always about speed. It's nice to have a varied repertoire of meals that include filling lasagnes, pies and casseroles, as well as the more obvious quick suppers such as pasta dishes, stir-fries and main-course salads.

Light Bites and Midweek Suppers – nutritious snacks and slightly more substantial dishes that are quick to make; serve with a green salad or follow with fruit.

Meals in Minutes – simple recipes that can be prepared, cooked and on the table within approximately 30 minutes. These are ideal for those nights when you don't have any leftovers to reuse but have time to pop into the supermarket for one or two key ingredients.

Cook Once, Eat Twice – these recipes take time and are usually cooked from scratch. You can make double the quantity and freeze half for an easy meal another day, or divide into portions and keep in the fridge for one or two family members to reheat later in the week.

Waste Not – we include tips on how to make the most of the bits & bobs that end up tucked away at the back of your fridge. Why waste leftovers when they can be transformed into another meal?

Before shopping

Before doing your weekly shop, have a good look at the ingredients in your fridge and vegetable rack and think of ways to use them up. You can then go out and buy the ingredients you need to make the most of your fridge items. For example:
• A half used pack of olives – add to a pasta dish, or to the Mozzarella, Parma Ham and Rocket Pizza on page 57
• A couple of rashers of bacon – perfect for making the Quick and Easy Carbonara on page 64
• A small piece of Camembert – perfect for making the Camembert and Tomato Tarts on page 34
• A couple of potatoes – perfect for topping the Lamb and Leek Hotpot on page 96

The weekly menu

This needn't be a hefty document – simply jot down an idea for every day of the week, including some dishes that you've already made and stored in the fridge or freezer, some recipes that make creative use of leftovers and some quick meals that need a trip to the shops for one or two fresh ingredients. Include vegetables or other accompaniments in your plan, but remember that you can always change your mind if you find a bargain in the supermarket.

Time savers

Use pre-prepared ingredients every now and again to save time in the kitchen. These can be bought fresh or be frozen and then thawed on the day of use:

Packs of chopped root vegetables
Perfect for casseroles
Prepared cauliflower and broccoli florets
Perfect for vegetable bakes such as the Cheese and Vegetable Bake (page 55)
Packs of chopped stir-fry vegetables
Perfect for stir-fries
Bags of washed and prepared salad
Perfect accompaniments, or use in the Throw-it-all-together Salad (page 39)
Frozen broad beans and peas
Perfect for making the Easy Pea Soup (page 45) and Spiced Egg Pilau (page 52)
Frozen fresh chopped herbs
Perfect for the Falafel, Rocket and Soured Cream Wraps (page 36) and the Chilli Bean Cake (page 54)
Ready-made garlic paste
Perfect for many recipes
Roasted vegetables in oil, such as red peppers, artichokes and sunblush or sun-dried tomatoes
Perfect for Mozzarella Mushrooms (page 32)
Jars of tomato sauce
Perfect for Aubergine Parmigiana (page 60) and Mozzarella, Parma Ham and Rocket Pizza (page 57)
Ready-rolled puff pastry
Perfect for Camembert and Tomato Tarts (page 34) and Express Apple Tart (page 117)

Making the most of your fridge, freezer and microwave

Having the right equipment can make life so much easier in the kitchen. Consider the space you have available: do you have room for a separate fridge and freezer? The microwave is energy-efficient, quick and easy to use – the busy cook's perfect kitchen companion.

The fridge

The fridge is a vital piece of equipment and keeps food fresh for longer. However, it is the main culprit for waste. The bigger it is, the more it becomes a repository for out-of-date condiments and bags of wilted salad leaves that lurk in its depths.

Safe storage
- Cool cooked food to room temperature before putting in the fridge
- Wrap or cover all food except fruit and vegetables
- Practise fridge discipline. The coldest shelves are at the bottom so store raw meat, fish and poultry there
- Separate cooked foods from raw foods

To make sure the fridge works properly:
- Don't overfill it
- Don't put hot foods in it
- Don't open the door more than necessary
- Clean it regularly

Vegetables and Fruit

Green vegetables	3–4 days
Salad leaves	2–3 days
Hard and stone fruit	3–7 days
Soft fruit	1–2 days

Dairy Food

Cheese, hard	1 week
Cheese, soft	2–3 days
Eggs	1 week
Milk	4–5 days

Fish

Fish	1 day
Shellfish	1 day

Raw Meat

Bacon	7 days
Game	2 days
Joints	3 days
Minced meat	1 day
Offal	1 day
Poultry	2 days
Raw sliced meat	2 days
Sausages	3 days

Cooked Meat

Joints	3 days
Casseroles/stews	2 days
Pies	2 days
Sliced meat	2 days
Ham	2 days
Ham, vacuum-packed (or according to the instructions on the pack)	1–2 weeks

The freezer

This is an invaluable storage tool and if you use it properly – particularly with batch cooking (see Cook Once, Eat Twice chapter) – you can save time and avoid wastage. Make sure you allow food time to thaw: if you leave it overnight in the fridge, your meal will be ready to pop into the oven when you get home from work. You can have all sorts of stand-bys waiting for you: breads, cakes, pastry, frozen vegetables and fruit such as raspberries and blackberries, cream, stocks, soups, herbs and bacon.

How to store food:
- Freeze food as soon as possible after purchase
- Label cooked food with the date and name of the dish
- Freeze food in portions
- Never put warm foods into the freezer, wait until they have cooled
- Check the manufacturer's instructions for freezing times
- Do not refreeze food once it has thawed

What not to store in the freezer:
- Whole eggs – freeze whites and yolks separately
- Fried foods – they lose their crispness and can go soggy
- Vegetables – cucumber, lettuce and celery have too high a water content
- Some sauces – mayonnaise and similar sauces will separate when thawed

To make sure the freezer works properly:
- Defrost it regularly
- Keep the freezer as full as possible

Thawing and reheating food:
Each recipe will give you instructions on how to reheat the particular dish, but generally:
- Some foods, such as vegetables, soups and sauces, can be cooked from frozen – dropped into boiling water, or heated gently in a pan until thawed
- Ensure other foods are thoroughly thawed before cooking
- Cook food as soon as possible after thawing
- Ensure the food is piping hot all the way through after cooking

The microwave

A conventional microwave oven cooks by microwaves that pass through glass, paper, china and plastic and are absorbed by moisture molecules in the food. They penetrate the food to a depth of about 5cm (2in), where they cause the molecules to vibrate and create heat within the food, which cooks it. The manufacturer's instruction booklet will tell you all you need to know to get the best out of the microwave oven, but here are a few handy tips:

Microwave safety:
- The oven will work only if the door is closed
- The door has a special seal to prevent microwaves from escaping
- Never switch on the microwave when there is nothing inside – the waves will bounce off the walls of the oven and could damage the magnetron (the device that converts electricity into microwaves)
- Allow sufficient space around the microwave for ventilation through the air vents
- If using plastic containers, use only microwave-proof plastic – ordinary plastic buckles

What to use a microwave for:
- Cooking ready-prepared meals
- Cooking vegetables and fish
- Reheating foods and drinks
- Softening butter and melting chocolate
- Drying herbs
- Scrambling eggs

What not to use a microwave for:
- Browning meat (unless the oven comes with a browning unit)
- Soufflés
- Puff pastry
- Breaded or battered foods

Microwave tips:
- Consult the manufacturer's handbook before you use the microwave for the first time
- Use a plastic trivet so that the microwaves can penetrate the underside of the food
- Cover fatty foods such as bacon and sausages with kitchen paper to soak up any fat
- Stir liquids at intervals during microwaving
- Turn large items of food over during microwaving
- Clean the interior regularly

Stocking your storecupboard

Dried

- ✓ Pasta and noodles
- ✓ Rice (long-grain, Arborio and other risotto rice, pudding rice)
- ✓ Pulses
- ✓ Pizza bases
- ✓ Nuts (pinenuts, walnuts, almonds)
- ✓ Dried fruits
- ✓ Stock cubes
- ✓ Spices and herbs
- ✓ Salt and pepper
- ✓ Flour (plain, self-raising, wholemeal and cornflour)
- ✓ Dried yeast
- ✓ Gelatine
- ✓ Baking powder, cream of tartar, bicarbonate of soda
- ✓ Sugar
- ✓ Tea
- ✓ Coffee
- ✓ Cocoa powder

Bottles and jars

- ✓ Mayonnaise
- ✓ Tomato ketchup and purée
- ✓ Tabasco sauce
- ✓ Worcestershire sauce
- ✓ Sweet chilli sauce
- ✓ Pasta sauces
- ✓ Thai fish sauce
- ✓ Curry paste
- ✓ Chutneys
- ✓ Pickles
- ✓ Olives
- ✓ Capers
- ✓ Mustards
- ✓ Oils
- ✓ Vinegar
- ✓ Jam
- ✓ Marmalade
- ✓ Honey

Cans

- ✓ Chopped and whole tomatoes
- ✓ Fish (salmon, tuna, anchovies)
- ✓ Beans, chickpeas and lentils
- ✓ Coconut milk/cream
- ✓ Fruits

The storecupboard

A well-stocked storecupboard can help you rustle up a quick meal at short notice. However, resist the urge to fill the cupboard with interesting bottles that you 'might use one day'.

A few rules on storage

- Keep food cupboards cool and dry
- Line shelves for easy cleaning and clean regularly
- Organize shelves – put new goods to the back and use up those in front
- Canned food, once opened, should be transferred to a bowl and kept in the fridge
- Store dried pulses, herbs, beans and spices in sealed containers. Light can affect these
- Check use-by dates regularly

Storecupboard Recipes

Storecupboard Omelette

a drizzle of olive oil or knob of butter, 1 large onion, finely chopped, 225g (8oz) cooked new potatoes, sliced, 125g (4oz) frozen petit pois, thawed, 6 eggs, beaten, 150g pack soft goat's cheese, sliced, salt and ground black pepper.

1 Heat the oil or butter in a 25.5cm (10in) non-stick, ovenproof frying pan. Add the onion and fry for 6–8 minutes until golden. Add the potatoes and petit pois and cook, stirring, for 2–3 minutes. Preheat the grill.

2 Spread the mixture over the base of the pan and pour in the eggs. Tilt the pan to coat the base with egg. Leave the omelette to cook undisturbed for 2–3 minutes, then top with the cheese.

3 Put the pan under the hot grill for 1–2 minutes until the egg is just set (no longer, or it will turn rubbery) and the cheese starts to turn golden. Season with salt and pepper and serve immediately.

Variations

- Use 100g (3¹/₂oz) sun-dried tomatoes instead of the new potatoes.
- Throw in a handful of halved pitted black olives as you pour the egg into the pan.

Storecupboard saviours

Here are some more ideas for recipes you can produce from a well-stocked storecupboard and just one or two fresh ingredients:

- Sticky Chicken Thighs (page 35)
- Spiced Egg Pilau (page 52)
- Warm Spicy Chorizo and Chickpea Salad (page 61)
- Moroccan Chicken with Chickpeas (page 95)

Mixed Beans with Lemon Vinaigrette

400g can mixed beans, drained and rinsed, 400g can chickpeas, drained and rinsed, 2 shallots, finely sliced, fresh mint sprigs and lemon zest to garnish
For the lemon vinaigrette
juice of 1 lemon, 2 tsp runny honey, 8 tbsp extra virgin olive oil, 3 tbsp freshly chopped mint, 4 tbsp roughly chopped flat-leafed parsley, salt and ground black pepper.

1 Put the beans, chickpeas and shallots in a large bowl.

2 To make the lemon vinaigrette, whisk together the lemon juice, seasoning and honey. Gradually whisk in the olive oil and stir in the chopped herbs.

3 Pour the vinaigrette over the bean mixture, toss well, then garnish with the mint sprigs and lemon zest and serve.

Ways of using leftovers

There are many ways of using leftover food and slightly over-ripe fruit and vegetables that are starting to wilt. You can:

- Simply add the ingredients to a stir-fry, pasta bake, soup, risotto ... the list is endless
- 'Stretch' the ingredients – sometimes the amount left over is so small it won't go very far in a family setting. Try adding to it. You can cook a little more of it (for example rice), or try adding lentils and tomatoes to leftover mince to create a whole new take on Bolognese sauce
- Make the most of fruit and vegetables that are starting to wilt – use fruit in a crumble, use vegetables in soups and bakes

The chart opposite gives some examples of typical fridge leftovers you could use in recipes in this book.

Expiry dates

These are a major area of debate. Supermarkets are extremely strict on expiry dates and will throw any food out the moment it is 'out of date'. Once you have purchased a product, you are asked to use it within the 'use by' date. After this, you are encouraged to throw it out and start again. However, with the odd exception – and using your judgement on certain danger foods like fish and eggs – you can simply check if it's okay to use by smell, look and feel. Follow your instincts, if it smells bad, bin it.

Using leftovers

We all struggle with portion sizing and often have some extra rice, potatoes or other ingredients left at the end of each meal. There is a difference between leftovers and waste food. Leftovers are the bits and pieces that sit in a clingfilm-covered bowl in your fridge, challenging you to use them creatively. If you ignore them for four or five days they become waste. Why not try making the most of your leftover bits & bobs?

How can I tell if my eggs are fresh?

A fresh egg should feel heavy in your hand and will sink to the bottom of the bowl or float on its side when put into water (1).
Older eggs, over two weeks old, will float vertically (2).

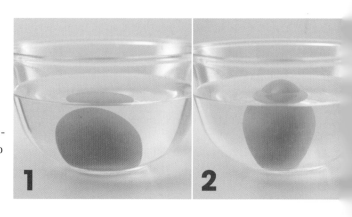

Planned leftovers

	First Use	Second Use	Third Use
Chicken	Perfect Roast Chicken (page 105)	Leftover Chicken Soup (below right) OR Throw-it-all-together Salad (page 39)	Chicken Stock (page 23)
Simple Bolognese Sauce	Spaghetti Bolognese (page 26)	Lasagne (page 26)	Cottage Pie (page 26)

Alternative suggestions

You may not always feel like transforming your leftovers into meals – or there may not be enough to do so. Another option is to freeze the odd ingredient for later use.

Small amounts of herbs – freeze in ice cube trays

One or two chillies – these freeze well and are easy to chop from frozen

Double cream – lightly whip the cream and then freeze

Cheese – hard cheeses will become crumbly once thawed, but can be used for grating or in cooking

Bread – whiz in a food processor to make breadcrumbs: these freeze well in a sealed plastic bag. Use to sprinkle over bakes for a crisp topping, or to coat fish or chicken before frying, grilling or baking – or use for bread sauce to serve with game or turkey

Versatile leftovers

Leftover	Recipe
Bowl of cooked pasta	Pasta with Pesto and Beans (page 53) Simple Salmon Pasta (page 65)
Bacon rashers	Quick and Easy Carbonara (page 64)
Mixed vegetables	Cheese and Vegetable Bake (page 55)
Savoy cabbage	Spanish-style Pork (page 87)
Salad	Throw-it-all together Salad (page 39)
Tomato sauce	Aubergine Parmigiana (page 60)
Over-ripe bananas	Instant Banana Ice Cream (page 115) Sticky Banoffee Pies (page 121)
Turning apples	Express Apple Tart (page 116)
Turning pears	Pear and Blackberry Crumble (page 112)
Fromage frais	Chicken with Spicy Couscous (page 75)
Custard	Cheat's Chocolate Pots (page 125)
Pancake batter	Chocolate Crêpes (page 111)

Leftover Roast Chicken Soup

3 tbsp olive oil, 1 onion, chopped, 1 carrot, chopped, 2 celery sticks, chopped, 2 fresh thyme sprigs, chopped, 1 bay leaf, a stripped roast chicken carcass, 900ml (1$\frac{1}{2}$ pints) boiling water, 150–200g (5–7oz) chopped roast chicken, 200g (7oz) mashed or roast potato, 1 tbsp double cream.

1 Heat the oil in a large pan. Add the onion, carrot, celery and thyme and fry gently for 20–30 minutes until soft but not brown. Add the bay leaf, chicken carcass and the boiling water to the pan. Bring to the boil, then simmer for 5 minutes.

2 Remove the bay leaf and carcass and add the chopped roast chicken and cooked potato. Simmer for 5 minutes.

3 Whiz the soup in a food processor, pour back into the pan and bring to the boil. Stir in the cream and serve immediately.

Cleaning

Before stuffing a chicken or other bird for roasting, clean it thoroughly. Put the bird in the sink and pull out any loose fat with your fingers. Run cold water through the cavity and dry the bird well using kitchen paper.

Roasting and carving chicken

A roast chicken has a luxurious aroma and flavour; it makes an excellent Sunday lunch or special meal with very little preparation. These simple guidelines make carving easy, giving neat slices to serve.

Roasting times

Roast for 20 minutes per 450g (1lb) plus 20 minutes at 180°C (160°C fan oven) mark 4.

How to check your chicken is cooked

Test by piercing the thickest part of the leg: the juices should run clear.

Carving

1 Starting at the neck end, cut slices about 5mm (¼in) thick.

2 To cut off the legs, cut the skin between the thigh and breast. Pull the leg down to expose the joint with the ribcage. Cut through that joint. (For small birds, cut through the joint between thigh and drumstick.)

3 To carve meat from the leg of large chickens, remove the leg from the carcass as above. Joint the two parts of the leg. Holding the drumstick by the thin end, stand it up on your carving board and carve slices parallel with the bone. Carve the thigh flat on the board or upright.

Preparing meat and poultry

Ready-prepared chicken pieces are perfect for midweek suppers, but a small bird doesn't take long to roast and is simple to prepare. Steaks and other cuts of meat can easily be made more tender and succulent for quick and tasty meals.

Hygiene

Raw poultry and meat contain harmful bacteria that can spread easily to anything they touch.
Always wash your hands, kitchen surfaces, chopping boards, knives and equipment before and after handling raw poultry or meat.
Don't let raw poultry or meat touch other foods.
Always cover raw poultry and meat, and store in the bottom of the fridge, where it can't touch or drip on to other foods.

1 3

Tenderising steak

Some cuts of steak benefit from tenderising. There are two ways to do it: by pounding or scoring.

1 To pound, lay the steaks in a single layer on a large piece of clingfilm or waxed paper. Lay another sheet on top of the slices and pound gently with a rolling pin, small frying pan or the flat side of a meat mallet.

2 Scoring is useful for cuts that have long, tough fibres, such as flank. It allows a marinade to penetrate more deeply into the meat. Lay the steak on the chopping board and, using a long, very sharp knife, make shallow cuts in one direction over the whole surface.

3 Make another set of cuts at a 45 degree angle to the first. Turn the meat over and repeat on the other side.

Trimming meat

When preparing meat for cutting into chunks, try to separate the individual muscles, which can be identified by the sinews running between each muscle.

Trimming a joint

1 Cut off the excess fat to leave a thickness of about 5mm (¼in) – a little fat will contribute juiciness and flavour. This isn't necessary for very lean cuts.

2 Trim away any stray pieces of meat or sinew left by the butcher.

3 If the joint has a covering of fat, you can lightly score it – taking care not to cut into the meat – to help the fat drain away during cooking.

Preparing vegetables

Nutritious, mouthwatering and essential to a healthy diet – vegetables are a must in every kitchen. Some vegetables turn brown after peeling, and need to be placed in acidulated water (water and lemon juice) to slow the discolouration down – the recipe will tell you when this is necessary.

Onions

1 Cut off the tip and base of the onion. Peel away all the layers of papery skin and any discoloured layers underneath.

2 Put the onion root end down on the chopping board, then, using a sharp knife, cut the onion in half from tip to base.

3 **Slicing** Put one half on the board with the cut surface facing down and slice across the onion.

4 **Chopping** Slice the halved onions from the root end to the top at regular intervals. Next, make 2–3 horizontal slices through the onion, then slice vertically across the width.

Shallots

1 Cut off the tip and trim off the ends of the root. Peel off the skin and any discoloured layers underneath.

2 Holding the shallot with the root end down, use a small sharp knife to make deep parallel slices almost down to the base while keeping the slices attached to it.

3 **Slicing** Turn the shallot on its side and cut off slices from the base.

4 **Dicing** Make deep parallel slices at right angles to the first slices. Turn it on its side and cut off the slices from the base. You should now have fine dice, but chop any larger pieces individually.

Peeling tomatoes

1 Fill a bowl or pan with boiling water. Using a slotted spoon, add the tomato for 15–30 seconds, then remove to a chopping board.

2 Use a small sharp knife to cut out the core in a single cone-shaped piece. Discard the core.

3 Peel off the skin; it should come away easily depending on ripeness.

Seeding unpeeled tomatoes

1 Halve the tomato through the core. Use a small sharp knife or a spoon to remove the seeds and juice. Shake off the excess liquid.

2 Chop the tomato as required for your recipe and place in a colander for a minute or two, to drain off any excess liquid.

Peppers

Red, green and yellow peppers all contain seeds and white pith which taste bitter and should be removed.
Cut the pepper in half vertically, discard the seeds and core, then trim away the rest of the white membrane with a small sharp knife. Alternatively, slice the top off the pepper, then cut away and discard the seeds and pith. Cut the pepper into strips or slices.

Leeks

As some leeks harbour a lot of grit and earth between their leaves, they need careful cleaning.

1 Cut off the root and any tough parts of the leek. Make a cut into the leaf end of the leek, about 7.5cm (3in) deep.

2 Hold under the cold tap while separating the cut halves to expose any grit. Wash well, then shake dry. Slice, cut into matchsticks or slice diagonally.

Celery

To remove the strings in the outer green stalks, trim the ends and cut into the base of the stalk with a small knife; catch the strings between the blade and your thumb. Pull up towards the top of the stalk to remove the string.

Mushrooms

Button, white, chestnut and flat mushrooms are all prepared in a similar way.
Shiitake mushrooms have a hard stalk; cut it off and use for making stock if you like.

1 Wipe with a damp cloth or pastry brush to remove any dirt.

2 With button mushrooms, cut off the stalk flush with the base of the cap. For other mushrooms, cut a thin disc off the end of the stalk and discard. Quarter or slice as needed.

Fennel

1 Trim off the top stems and the base of the bulbs. Remove the core with a small sharp knife if it is tough.

2 The outer leaves may be discoloured and can be scrubbed gently in cold water, or you can peel away the discoloured parts with a knife or a vegetable peeler. Slice or chop the fennel.

Making stock

Good stock can make the difference between a good dish and a great one. It gives depth of flavour to many dishes. There are four main types of stock: vegetable, meat, chicken and fish.

Stocks

Vegetable stock

For 1.1 litres (2 pints), you will need:
225g (8oz) each onions, celery, leeks and carrots, chopped, 2 bay leaves, a few thyme sprigs, 1 small bunch parsley, 10 black peppercorns, ½ tsp salt.

1 Put all the ingredients in a pan and pour in 1.7 litres (3 pints) cold water. Bring slowly to the boil and skim the surface. Partially cover and simmer for 30 minutes. Adjust the seasoning. Strain the stock through a fine sieve and leave to cool.

Meat stock

For 1.1 litres (2 pints), you will need:
450g (1lb) each meat bones and stewing meat, 1 onion, 2 celery sticks and 1 large carrot, sliced, 1 bouquet garni (2 bay leaves, a few thyme sprigs and a small bunch parsley), 1 tsp black peppercorns, ½ tsp salt.

1 Preheat the oven to 220°C (200°C fan oven) mark 7. Put the meat and bones in a roasting tin and roast for 30–40 minutes, turning now and again, until they are well browned.

2 Put the bones in a large pan with the remaining ingredients and add 2 litres (3½ pints) cold water. Bring slowly to the boil and skim the surface. Partially cover and simmer for 4–5 hours. Adjust the seasoning.

3 Strain the stock through a muslin-lined sieve into a bowl and cool quickly. Degrease (see opposite) before using.

Chicken stock

For 1.1 litres (2 pints), you will need:
1.6kg (3¹/₂lb) chicken bones or a stripped roast chicken carcass, 225g (8oz) each onions and celery, sliced, 150g (5oz) chopped leeks, 1 bouquet garni (2 bay leaves, a few thyme sprigs and a small bunch parsley), 1 tsp black peppercorns, ¹/₂ tsp salt.

1 Put all the ingredients in a large pan with 3 litres (5¹/₄ pints) cold water.

2 Bring slowly to the boil and skim the surface. Partially cover the pan and simmer gently for 2 hours. Adjust the seasoning if necessary.

3 Strain the stock through a muslin-lined sieve into a bowl and cool quickly. Degrease (see right) before using.

Fish stock

For 900ml (1¹/₂ pints), you will need:
900g (2lb) fish bones and trimmings, washed, 2 carrots, 1 onion and 2 celery sticks, sliced, 1 bouquet garni (2 bay leaves, a few thyme sprigs and a small bunch parsley), 6 white peppercorns, ¹/₂ tsp salt.

1 Put all the ingredients in a large pan with 900ml (1¹/₂ pints) cold water. Bring slowly to the boil and skim the surface.

2 Partially cover the pan and simmer gently for 30 minutes. Adjust the seasoning if necessary.

3 Strain through a muslin-lined sieve into a bowl and cool quickly. Fish stock tends not to have much fat in it and so does not usually need to be degreased. However, if it does seem to be fatty, you will need to remove this by degreasing it (see right).

Degreasing stock

Meat and poultry stock needs to be degreased. (Vegetable stock does not.) You can mop the fat from the surface using kitchen paper, but the following methods are easier and more effective. There are three main methods that you can use: ladling, pouring and chilling.

1 **Ladling** While the stock is warm, place a ladle on the surface. Press down to allow the fat floating on the surface to trickle over the edge until the ladle is full. Discard the fat, then repeat until all the fat has been removed.

2 **Pouring** For this you need a degreasing jug or a double-pouring gravy boat, which has the spout at the base of the vessel. When you fill the jug or gravy boat with a fatty liquid, the fat rises. When you pour, the stock comes out while the fat stays behind in the jug.

3 **Chilling** This technique works best with stock made from meat, whose fat solidifies when cold. Put the stock in the fridge until the fat becomes solid, then remove the pieces of fat using a slotted spoon.

Cooking rice, pasta, grains and potatoes

Wholesome and healthy, rice, grains and potatoes are everyday staples. Easy to prepare and cook, they are also very economical and they store well.

Cooking rice

There are two main types of rice: long-grain and short-grain. Long-grain rice is generally served as an accompaniment; the most commonly used type of long-grain rice in South-east Asian cooking is jasmine rice, also known as Thai fragrant rice. It has a distinctive taste and slightly sticky texture. Long-grain rice needs no special preparation, although it should be washed to remove excess starch. Put the rice in a bowl and cover with cold water. Stir until this becomes cloudy, then drain and repeat until the water is clear.

Long-grain rice

1 Use 50–75g (2–3oz) raw rice per person; measured by volume 50–75ml (2–2½fl oz). Measure the rice by volume and put it in a pan with a pinch of salt and twice the volume of boiling water (or stock).

2 Bring to the boil. Turn the heat down to low and set the timer for the time stated on the pack. The rice should be al dente: tender with a bite at the centre.

3 When the rice is cooked, fluff up the grains with a fork.

Perfect rice

If you cook rice often, you may want to invest in a special rice steamer. They are available in Asian supermarkets and some kitchen shops and give good, consistent results.

Cooking pasta

Use about 1 litre (1³/₄ pints) of water per 100g (3¹/₂oz) of pasta. Filled pasta is the only type of pasta that needs oil in the cooking water – the oil reduces friction, which could tear the wrappers and allow the filling to come out. If the recipe calls for cooking the pasta with a sauce after it has boiled, undercook the pasta slightly when boiling it. Rinse pasta after cooking only if you are going to cool it to use in a salad, then drain well and toss with oil.

Dried pasta

1 Heat the water with about 1 tsp salt per 100g (3¹/₂oz) of pasta. Bring to a rolling boil, then add all the pasta and stir well for 30 seconds, to keep the pasta from sticking.

2 Once the water is boiling again, set the timer for 2 minutes less than the cooking time on the pack and cook uncovered.

3 Check the pasta when the timer goes off, then every 60 seconds until it is cooked al dente: tender, but with a bite at the centre. Drain in a colander.

Fresh pasta

Fresh pasta is cooked in the same way as dried, but for a shorter time. Bring the water to the boil. Add the pasta to the boiling water all at once and stir well. Set the timer for 2 minutes and keep testing every 30 seconds until the pasta is cooked al dente: tender, but with a bite at the centre. Drain in a colander.

Couscous

Often mistaken for a grain, couscous is actually a type of pasta that originated in North Africa. It is perfect for making into salads or serving with stews and casseroles. The tiny pellets do not require cooking and can simply be soaked.

1 Measure the couscous in a jug and add 1¹/₂ times the volume of just-boiled water or stock.

2 Cover the bowl and leave to soak for 5 minutes. Fluff up with a fork before serving.

3 If using for a salad, leave the couscous to cool completely before adding the other salad ingredients.

Boiling potatoes

1 Peel or scrub old potatoes, scrape or scrub new potatoes. Cut large potatoes into even-sized chunks and put them in a pan with plenty of salted cold water.

2 Cover, bring to the boil, then reduce the heat and simmer until cooked – about 10 minutes for new potatoes, 15–20 minutes for old.

Mashed Potatoes

For four people, you will need:
900g (2lb) floury potatoes such as Maris Piper, 125ml (4fl oz) full-fat milk, 25g (1oz) butter, salt and ground black pepper.

1 Peel the potatoes and cut into even-sized chunks. Boil as above until just tender, 15–20 minutes. Test with a small knife. Drain well.

2 Put the potatoes back in the pan and cover with a clean teatowel for 5 minutes, or warm them over a very low heat until the moisture has evaporated.

3 Pour the milk into a small pan and bring to the boil. Pour on to the potatoes with the butter and season.

4 Mash the potatoes until smooth.

Simple Bolognese Sauce

This sauce tastes even better the day after it's been made.
1 tbsp olive oil, 1 large onion, finely chopped, 1 carrot,
finely chopped, 1 celery stick, finely chopped, 1 garlic
clove, crushed, 125g (4oz) button mushrooms, chopped,
450g (1lb) minced meat, 300ml (½ pint) stock, 300ml
(½ pint) red or dry white wine, 400g can chopped
tomatoes, 1 tbsp tomato purée, 2 tsp dried oregano, 2 tbsp
freshly chopped parsley, salt and ground black pepper.
To serve freshly cooked pasta, freshly grated Parmesan.

1 Heat the oil in a frying pan. Add the onion, carrot,
celery and garlic and fry gently for 5 minutes or until
soft. Add the mushrooms and fry for a further minute.

2 Stir in the meat and cook, stirring, over a high heat
until browned. Stir in the stock, wine, tomatoes,
tomato purée, oregano and seasoning. Bring to the
boil, cover and simmer for 1 hour or until the meat is
tender and the sauce is well reduced.

3 Adjust the seasoning and stir in the parsley before
serving with pasta and Parmesan.

Variations

Cottage Pie Preheat the oven to 200°C (180°C fan oven)
mark 6. Add 1 tbsp plain flour once the meat has browned.
Omit the tomatoes and add 450ml (¾ pint) beef stock. Add
1 medium carrot, diced, with the mushrooms. Spoon the
sauce into a 1.7 litre (3 pint) ovenproof dish and top with
1kg (2¼lb) mashed potato. Cook for 20–25 minutes.
Lasagne Preheat the oven to 200°C (180°C fan oven) mark
6. When the bolognese sauce is nearly finished, make a
double quantity of cheese sauce (page 55). Spoon half the
bolognese sauce into a shallow 1.7 litre (3 pint) ovenproof
dish. Top with 2 sheets of lasagne (the 'no precooking
required' type) and half the cheese sauce. Repeat with the
rest of the bolognese, lasagne and cheese sauce. Sprinkle with
1 tbsp grated cheese. Cook for 35 minutes.
Chilli con Carne After cooking the vegetables for
5 minutes, add 1 seeded, chopped red pepper and cook
for a further 5 minutes. Add 2 tsp mild chilli powder with
the mince. Drain a 400g can of red kidney beans and add
to the pan for the final 5 minutes of cooking time. Serve
with rice, jacket potatoes or in a flour tortilla. Grate some
Cheddar cheese over, if you like.
'Stretch' the mince Replace half the mince with 200g
(7oz) red lentils and add them after browning the mince.
There's no need to soak them, just stir them in.

Making sauces

If you're cooking a sauce for a meal, it makes
sense to cook double the quantity and freeze
half. Once you've made a big batch, you can
create speedy midweek meals that are all
different! A simple tomato or Bolognese sauce
can be the basis for many a warming treat. Pasta
is always a great standby for a quick supper –
here's a handful of ideas for when you're short
of time or inspiration.

Eight quick pasta sauces

Tomato and Basil

Heat 1 tbsp olive oil in a pan, add 3 crushed garlic cloves and cook for 30 seconds only. Add a 500g carton creamed tomatoes or passata, 1 bay leaf and 1 thyme sprig. Season with salt and ground black pepper and add a large pinch of sugar. Bring to the boil, then reduce the heat and simmer, uncovered, for 5–10 minutes. Remove the bay leaf and thyme and add 3 tbsp freshly chopped basil.

Tomato, Prawn and Garlic

Put 350g (12oz) cooked peeled prawns in a bowl with 4 tbsp sun-dried tomato paste and stir well. Heat 1 tbsp olive oil and 15g ($\frac{1}{2}$ oz) butter in a frying pan and gently cook 3 sliced garlic cloves until golden. Add 4 large chopped tomatoes and 125ml (4fl oz) dry white wine. Leave the sauce to bubble for about 5 minutes, then stir in the prawns and 20g ($^3/_4$oz) freshly chopped parsley.

Creamy Pesto

Put 5 tbsp freshly grated Parmesan, 25g (1oz) toasted pinenuts, 200g carton low-fat fromage frais and 2 garlic cloves into a food processor. Whiz to a thick paste. Season generously with salt and ground black pepper. Add 40g (1$^1/_2$oz) each torn fresh basil leaves and roughly chopped fresh parsley and whiz for 2–3 seconds.

Lemon and Parmesan

Cook pasta shells in a large pan of boiling salted water for the time stated on the pack. Add 125g (4oz) frozen petit pois to the pasta water for the last 5 minutes of the cooking time. Drain the pasta and peas, put back in the pan and add the grated zest and juice of $\frac{1}{2}$ lemon and 75g (3oz) freshly grated Parmesan. Season with ground black pepper, toss and serve immediately.

Mushroom and Cream

Heat 1 tbsp olive oil in a large pan and fry 1 finely chopped onion for 7–10 minutes until soft. Add 300g (11oz) sliced mushrooms and cook for 3–4 minutes. Pour in 125ml (4fl oz) dry white wine and bubble for 1 minute, then stir in 500ml (18fl oz) low-fat crème fraîche. Heat until bubbling, then stir in 2 tbsp freshly chopped tarragon. Season with salt and ground black pepper.

Courgette and Anchovy

Heat the oil from a 50g can anchovies in a frying pan. Add 1 crushed garlic clove and a pinch of dried chilli and cook for 1 minute. Add 400ml (14fl oz) passata, 2 diced courgettes and the anchovies. Bring to the boil, then reduce the heat and simmer for about 10 minutes, stirring well, until the anchovies have melted.

Walnut and Creamy Blue Cheese

Heat 1 tsp olive oil in a small pan, add 1 crushed garlic clove and 25g (1oz) toasted walnut pieces and cook for 1 minute – the garlic should just be golden. Add 100g (3$^1/_2$oz) cubed Gorgonzola and 150ml ($^1/_4$ pint) single cream. Season with ground black pepper.

Broccoli and Thyme

Put 900g (2lb) trimmed tenderstem broccoli in a pan with 150ml ($^1/_4$ pint) hot vegetable stock. Bring to the boil, then cover and simmer for 3–4 minutes until tender – the stock should have evaporated. Add 2 crushed garlic cloves and 2 tbsp olive oil and cook for 1–2 minutes to soften the garlic. Add 250g carton mascarpone, 2 tbsp freshly chopped thyme and 100g (3$^1/_2$oz) freshly grated pecorino cheese and mix together. Season with salt and ground black pepper.

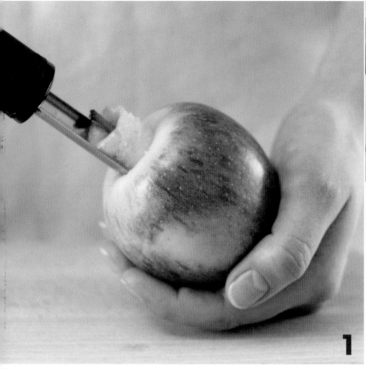

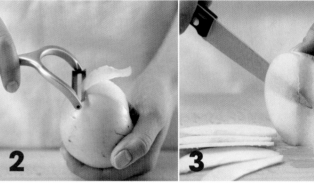

Preparing fruit

Soft fruits – strawberries, blackberries, raspberries and currants – are generally quick to prepare. Always handle ripe fruits gently as they can be delicate.

Apples

1 **To core** an apple, push an apple corer straight through the apple from the stem the base. Remove the core and use a small sharp knife to pick out any stray seeds or seed casings.

2 **To peel**, hold the fruit in one hand and run a swivel peeler under the skin, starting from the stem end and moving around the fruit, taking off the skin until you reach the base.

3 **To slice**, halve the cored apple. For flat slices, hold the apple cut side down and slice with the knife blade at right angles to the hollow left by the core. For crescent-shaped slices, stand the fruit on its end and cut slices into the hollow as if you were slicing a pie.

Pears

1 **To core**, use a teaspoon to scoop out the seeds and core through the base of the pear. Trim away any remaining fragments with a small knife. If you halve or quarter the pear, remove any remaining seeds.

2 **To peel**, cut off the stem. Peel off the skin in even strips from tip to base. If not using immediately, toss the pears in lemon juice.

3 **To slice**, halve the cored, peeled pear lengthways. Check for any remaining fragments of core, then slice with the pear halves lying cut side down on the board.

4 **To make pear fans**, slice at closely spaced intervals from the base to about 2.5cm (1in) from the tip, making sure you don't cut all the way through.

Berries

Most soft fruits can be washed very gently in cold water. Shop-bought blackberries will usually have the hull removed. If you have picked blackberries yourself the hulls and stalks may still be attached, so pick over the berries carefully and remove any that remain. Raspberries are very delicate so handle very carefully; remove any stalks and hulls. Leave strawberries whole.

1 Place the berries in a bowl of cold water and allow any small pieces of grit, dust or insects to float out.

2 Transfer the fruit to a colander and rinse gently under fresh running water. Drain well, then leave to drain on kitchen paper.

Hulling strawberries

1 Wash the strawberries gently and dry on kitchen paper. Remove the hull (the centre part that was attached to the plant) from the strawberry using a strawberry huller or a small sharp knife.

2 Put the knife into the small, hard area beneath the green stalk and gently rotate to remove a small, cone-shaped piece.

Stripping currants

Blackcurrants, redcurrants and whitecurrants can all be stripped quickly and simply from the stem in the same way.

1 Using a fork, strip all the currants off the stalks by running the fork down the length of the stalk.

2 Put the currants into a colander and wash them gently.

1

2

Mangoes

1 Cut a slice to one side of the stone in the centre. Repeat on the other side.

2 Cut parallel lines into the flesh of one slice, almost to the skin. Cut another set of lines to cut the flesh into squares.

3 Press on the skin side to turn the fruit inside out, so that the flesh is thrust outwards. Cut off the chunks as close as possible to the skin. Repeat with the other half.

1

2

3

1

Light Bites

Mozzarella Mushrooms

8 large portobello mushrooms

8 slices marinated red pepper

8 fresh basil leaves

150g (5oz) mozzarella, cut into 8 slices

4 English muffins, halved

salt and ground black pepper

green salad to serve

1 Preheat the oven to 200°C (180°C fan oven) mark 6. Lay the mushrooms side by side in a roasting tin and season with salt and pepper. Top each mushroom with a slice of red pepper and a basil leaf. Lay a slice of mozzarella on top of each mushroom. Season again. Roast in the oven for 15–20 minutes until the mushrooms are tender and the cheese has melted.

2 Meanwhile, toast the muffin halves until golden. Put a mozzarella mushroom on top of each muffin half. Serve immediately with a green salad.

Serves	EASY		NUTRITIONAL INFORMATION	
4	**Preparation Time** 2–3 minutes	**Cooking Time** 15–20 minutes	**Per Serving** 137 calories, 8.5g fat (of which 5g saturates), 5g carbohydrate, 0.4g salt	Vegetarian

Cook's Tips

Chillies vary enormously in strength, from quite mild to blisteringly hot, depending on the type of chilli and its ripeness. Taste a small piece first to check it's not too hot for you.

Be extremely careful when handling chillies not to touch or rub your eyes with your fingers, or they will sting. Wash knives immediately after handling chillies. As a precaution, use rubber gloves when preparing them, if you like.

Waste Not

Use leftover bread to make breadcrumbs and freeze – a great timesaver. You can use them from frozen.

200g (7oz) fresh crabmeat

2 spring onions, finely chopped

2 red chillies, seeded and finely chopped (see Cook's Tips)

finely grated zest of 1 lime

4 tbsp freshly chopped coriander

about 40g (1½oz) wholemeal breadcrumbs

1 tbsp groundnut oil

1 tbsp plain flour

salt and ground black pepper

thinly sliced red chilli, seeds removed, to garnish

1 lime, cut into wedges, and salad leaves to serve

Quick Crab Cakes

1 Put the crabmeat in a bowl, then mix with the spring onions, chillies, lime zest, coriander and seasoning. Add enough breadcrumbs to hold the mixture together, then form into four small patties.

2 Heat ½ tbsp groundnut oil in a pan. Dredge the patties with flour and fry on one side for 3 minutes. Add the remaining oil, then turn the patties over and fry for a further 2–3 minutes. Garnish the crab cakes with thinly sliced red chilli and serve with lime wedges to squeeze over them, and salad leaves.

EASY		NUTRITIONAL INFORMATION		Serves
Preparation Time 15 minutes	**Cooking Time** 6 minutes	**Per Serving** 124 calories, 4g fat (of which 1g saturates), 12g carbohydrate, 0.9g salt	Dairy free	**4**

Cook's Tip

Originally from Provence in southern France, tapenade is a strongly flavoured paste made from black olives, capers, anchovies, garlic and olive oil.

Camembert and Tomato Tarts

½ x 375g pack ready-rolled puff pastry

2 tbsp tapenade (see Cook's Tip)

200g (7oz) cherry tomatoes, halved

75g (3oz) Camembert, sliced
salad to serve

1 Preheat the oven to 220°C (200°C fan oven) mark 7. Cut the puff pastry into four pieces. Score a border and prick the pastry inside the border with a fork. Put on to a baking sheet and cook for 8–10 minutes until risen.

2 Press down the centre of each tart slightly with the back of a fish slice, then spread with the tapenade. Top with the tomatoes and sliced Camembert. Put back into the oven for a further 7–8 minutes until golden brown. Serve warm with salad.

Serves 4	EASY		NUTRITIONAL INFORMATION
	Preparation Time 10 minutes	**Cooking Time** 15–20 minutes	**Per Serving** 253 calories, 17g fat (of which 4g saturates), 19g carbohydrate, 1.1g salt

Try Something Different

Try this with sausages instead of the chicken.
Italian marinade Mix 1 crushed garlic clove with 4 tbsp olive oil, the juice of 1 lemon and 1 tsp dried oregano. If you like, leave to marinate for 1–2 hours before cooking.
Oriental marinade Mix together 2 tbsp soy sauce, 1 tsp demerara sugar, 2 tbsp dry sherry or apple juice, 1 tsp finely chopped fresh root ginger and 1 crushed garlic clove.
Honey and mustard Mix together 2 tbsp grain mustard, 3 tbsp clear honey and the grated zest and juice of 1 lemon.

Sticky Chicken Thighs

1 garlic clove, crushed
1 tbsp clear honey
1 tbsp Thai sweet chilli sauce
4 chicken thighs
green salad to serve

1 Preheat the oven to 200°C (180°C fan oven) mark 6. Put the garlic into a bowl with the honey and chilli sauce and mix together. Add the chicken thighs and toss to coat.

2 Put into a roasting tin and roast for 15–20 minutes until the chicken is golden and cooked through. Serve with a crisp green salad.

EASY		NUTRITIONAL INFORMATION		Serves
Preparation Time 5 minutes	**Cooking Time** 20 minutes	**Per Serving** 218 calories, 12g fat (of which 3g saturates), 5g carbohydrate, 0.4g salt	Gluten free Dairy free	**4**

Falafel, Rocket and Soured Cream Wraps

6 large flour tortillas
200g (7oz) soured cream
100g (3½oz) wild rocket
a small handful of fresh coriander, chopped
1 celery stick, finely chopped
180g pack ready-made falafel, roughly chopped or crumbled

1 Lay the tortillas on a board and spread each one with a little soured cream.

2 Divide the rocket among the wraps and sprinkle with coriander, celery and falafel.

3 Roll up as tightly as you can, then wrap each roll in clingfilm and chill for up to 3 hours or until ready to use. To serve, unwrap and cut each roll into quarters.

Serves 6	EASY		NUTRITIONAL INFORMATION	
	Preparation Time 5 minutes, plus chilling		**Per Serving** 270 calories, 8.8g fat (of which 4.4g saturates), 42.1g carbohydrate, 0.5g salt	Vegetarian

Cook's Tip

Miso (fermented barley and soya beans) contains beneficial live enzymes that can be destroyed by boiling. Miso is best added as a flavouring at the end of cooking. It's available from Asian shops, health-food shops and larger supermarkets.

Mushroom, Spinach and Miso Soup

1 tbsp vegetable oil

1 onion, finely sliced

125g (4oz) shiitake mushrooms, finely sliced

225g (8oz) baby spinach leaves

1.1 litres (2 pints) vegetable or chicken stock

4 tbsp mugi miso (see Cook's Tip)

1 Heat the oil in a large pan over a low heat. Add the onion and cook gently for 15 minutes or until soft.

2 Add the mushrooms and cook for 5 minutes, then stir in the spinach and stock. Heat for 3 minutes, then stir in the miso – don't boil, as miso is a live culture (see Cook's Tip). Spoon the soup into warmed bowls and serve hot.

Serves	EASY		NUTRITIONAL INFORMATION	
6	**Preparation Time** 5 minutes	**Cooking Time** 25 minutes	**Per Serving** 55 calories, 2g fat (of which trace saturates), 6g carbohydrate, 1.3g salt	Dairy free

Cook's Tips

Use leftover roast chicken or beef, or cooked ham for this recipe.

Use washed and prepared salad instead of Chinese leaves and watercress.

4 chargrilled chicken breasts, about 125g (4oz) each, torn into strips

2 carrots, cut into strips

$1/_2$ cucumber, halved lengthways, seeded and cut into ribbons

a handful of fresh coriander leaves, roughly chopped

$1/_2$ head of Chinese leaves, shredded

4 handfuls of watercress

4 spring onions, shredded

For the dressing

5 tbsp peanut butter

2 tbsp sweet chilli sauce

juice of 1 lime

salt and ground black pepper

Throw-it-all-together Salad

1 Put the chicken strips and all the salad ingredients into a large salad bowl.

2 To make the dressing, put the peanut butter, chilli sauce and lime juice in a small bowl and mix together well. Season with salt and pepper. If the dressing is too thick to pour, add 2–3 tbsp cold water, a tablespoon at a time, to thin it – use just enough water to make the dressing the correct consistency.

3 Drizzle the dressing over the salad, toss gently together and serve.

EASY	NUTRITIONAL INFORMATION		Serves
Preparation Time 10 minutes	**Per Serving** 215 calories, 9g fat (of which 2g saturates), 9g carbohydrate, 0.6g salt	Gluten free Dairy free	**4**

Tomato Crostini with Feta and Basil

1 small garlic clove, crushed

3 tbsp freshly chopped basil, plus extra basil leaves to garnish

25g (1oz) pinenuts

2 tbsp extra virgin olive oil

grated zest and juice of 1 lime

50g (2oz) feta cheese

4 large tomatoes, vine-ripened if possible, thickly sliced

150g carton fresh tomato salsa

50g (2oz) pitted black olives, roughly chopped

4 thick slices country-style bread

salt and ground black pepper

1 Whiz the garlic, basil, pinenuts, olive oil, lime zest and juice together in a food processor to form a smooth paste. Alternatively, use a mortar and pestle. Add the feta cheese and blend until smooth. Thin with 1 tbsp water if necessary. Season with salt and pepper.

2 Put the tomatoes, salsa and olives in a bowl and gently toss together.

3 Toast the bread. Divide the tomato mixture among the slices of toast and spoon the basil and feta mixture over the top. Garnish with basil leaves and serve.

Serves	EASY		NUTRITIONAL INFORMATION
4	**Preparation Time** 20 minutes	**Cooking Time** 3 minutes	**Per Serving** 242 calories, 17g fat (of which 3g saturates), 18g carbohydrate, 1.5g salt

Cook's Tips

Use leftover bread for this tasty brunch dish.
For a savoury version, use white bread and omit the spice and sugar; serve with tomato ketchup, or with bacon and maple syrup.

2 medium eggs

150ml (¼ pint) semi-skimmed milk

a generous pinch of freshly grated nutmeg or ground cinnamon

4 slices white bread, or fruit bread, crusts removed and each slice cut into four fingers

50g (2oz) butter

vegetable oil for frying

1 tbsp golden caster sugar

French Toast

1 Beat the eggs, milk and nutmeg or cinnamon together in a shallow dish.

2 Dip the pieces of bread into the mixture, coating them well.

3 Heat half the butter with 1 tbsp oil in a heavy-based frying pan. When the butter is foaming, fry the egg-coated bread pieces in batches, until golden on both sides, adding more butter and oil as needed. Sprinkle with sugar to serve for brunch.

EASY		NUTRITIONAL INFORMATION		Serves
Preparation Time 5 minutes	**Cooking Time** 10 minutes	**Per Finger** 259 calories, 19.6g fat (of which 8.6g saturates), 15.2g carbohydrate, 0.7g salt	Vegetarian	**4**

Scrambled Eggs with Smoked Salmon

6 large eggs

25g (1oz) butter, plus extra to spread

100g (3¹/₂oz) mascarpone

125g pack smoked salmon, sliced, or smoked salmon trimmings

6 slices sourdough or rye bread, toasted, buttered and cut into slim rectangles for soldiers

salt and ground black pepper

1 Crack the eggs into a jug and lightly beat together. Season well.

2 Melt the butter in a non-stick pan over a low heat. Add the eggs and stir constantly until the mixture thickens. Add the mascarpone and season well. Cook for 1–2 minutes longer, until the mixture just becomes firm, then fold in the smoked salmon. Serve at once with toasted bread soldiers.

EASY		NUTRITIONAL INFORMATION	Serves
Preparation Time 10 minutes	**Cooking Time** 5 minutes	**Per Serving** 457 calories, 33.9g fat (of which 17.3g saturates), 17.2g carbohydrate, 2.7g salt	4

Croque Monsieur

4 slices white bread

butter, softened, to spread, plus extra for frying

Dijon mustard, to taste

125g (4oz) Gruyère cheese

4 slices ham

1 Spread each slice of bread on both sides with the butter. Then spread one side of two slices of bread with a little Dijon mustard.

2 Divide the cheese and ham between the two mustard-spread bread slices. Put the other slice of bread on top and press down.

3 Heat a griddle with a little butter until hot and fry the sandwiches for 2–3 minutes on each side until golden and crispy and the cheese starts to melt.

4 Slice in half and serve immediately.

Serves	EASY		NUTRITIONAL INFORMATION
2	**Preparation Time** 5 minutes	**Cooking Time** 8 minutes	**Per Serving** 551 calories, 35.4g fat (of which 22.4g saturates), 27.2g carbohydrate, 3.6g salt

Easy Pea Soup

1 small baguette, thinly sliced

2 tbsp basil-infused olive oil, plus extra to drizzle

450g (1lb) frozen peas, thawed

600ml (1 pint) vegetable stock

salt and ground black pepper

1 Preheat the oven to 220°C (200°C fan oven) mark 7. To make the croûtons, put the baguette slices on a baking sheet, drizzle with 2 tbsp basil oil and cook in the oven for 10–15 minutes until golden.

2 Meanwhile, put the peas in a food processor or blender, add the stock and season with salt and pepper. Whiz for 2–3 minutes.

3 Pour the soup into a pan and bring to the boil, then reduce the heat and simmer for 10 minutes. Spoon into warmed bowls, add the croûtons, drizzle with extra oil and sprinkle with salt and pepper. Serve immediately.

EASY		NUTRITIONAL INFORMATION		Serves
Preparation Time 2 minutes, plus thawing	**Cooking Time** 15 minutes	**Per Serving** 408 calories, 9g fat (of which 2g saturates), 69g carbohydrate, 1.8g salt	Vegetarian Dairy free	**6**

Cook's Tip

You can use any type of bread for this recipe.

Cheesy Tuna Melt

2 slices cholla bread
100g can tuna in sunflower oil, drained
75g (3oz) Gruyère cheese, sliced
1 tomato, sliced
salt and ground black pepper

1 Preheat the grill to high. Put the bread on a baking sheet and toast one side.

2 Turn the bread so that it is untoasted side up, then divide the tuna between the two pieces and add the cheese and tomato.

3 Grill until the cheese is bubbling and golden. Season with salt and pepper and serve immediately.

Serves	EASY		NUTRITIONAL INFORMATION
1	**Preparation Time** 5 minutes	**Cooking Time** 5 minutes	**Per Serving** 747 calories, 35.6g fat (of which 18.1g saturates), 51.4g carbohydrate, 3.4g salt

Cook's Tip

Frozen seafood mix is a useful standby. Use it instead of the fish and shellfish in this recipe but take care not to overcook or it will become tough.

1 leek, finely sliced

4 fat garlic cloves, crushed

3 celery sticks, finely sliced

1 small fennel bulb, finely sliced

1 red chilli, seeded and finely chopped (see page 33)

3 tbsp olive oil

50ml (2fl oz) dry white wine

about 750g (1lb 10oz) mixed fish and shellfish, such as haddock, monkfish, salmon, raw shelled prawns and cleaned mussels

4 medium tomatoes, chopped

2 tbsp freshly chopped thyme

salt and ground black pepper

Fast Fish Soup

1 Put the leek in a large pan and add the garlic, celery, fennel, chilli and olive oil. Cook over a medium heat for 5 minutes or until the vegetables are soft and beginning to colour.

2 Stir in 1.1 litres (2 pints) boiling water and the wine. Bring to the boil, then simmer the soup, covered, for 5 minutes.

3 Meanwhile, cut the fish into large chunks. Add to the soup with the tomatoes and thyme. Continue simmering gently until the fish has just turned opaque. Add the prawns and simmer for 1 minute then add the mussels – if you're using them. As soon as all the mussels have opened, season the soup and ladle into warmed bowls. Discard any mussels that remain closed, then serve immediately.

EASY		NUTRITIONAL INFORMATION		Serves
Preparation Time 10 minutes	**Cooking Time** 15 minutes	**Per Serving** 269 calories, 10g fat (of which 2g saturates), 6g carbohydrate, 0.6g salt	Gluten free Dairy free	**4**

2

Midweek Suppers

Speedy Beef Noodles

250g (9oz) fine egg noodles

4 tbsp sesame oil, plus a little extra to brush

300g (11oz) beef fillet

4 tbsp chilli soy sauce

juice of 1 lime

2 red peppers, halved, seeded and cut into thin strips

200g (7oz) mangetouts, sliced

4 tbsp freshly chopped coriander

1 Put the noodles in a large bowl and cover with boiling water. Leave to soak for 4 minutes, then rinse under cold running water and set aside.

2 Meanwhile, brush a large frying pan or griddle with a little sesame oil and heat until hot. Fry the beef for 3–4 minutes on each side, or 4–5 minutes if you like it well done. Remove from the pan and keep warm.

3 Add the 4 tbsp sesame oil to the pan with the chilli soy sauce, lime juice, red peppers, mangetouts and coriander and stir to mix. Add the noodles and use two large spoons to toss them over the heat to combine with the sauce and warm through.

4 Cut the beef into thin slices and serve on a bed of noodles.

Serves	EASY		NUTRITIONAL INFORMATION	
4	**Preparation Time** 5 minutes	**Cooking Time** 10 minutes	**Per Serving** 510 calories, 19g fat (of which 5g saturates), 60g carbohydrate, 2.8g salt	Dairy free

Spiced Egg Pilau

200g (7oz) basmati or wild rice
150g (5oz) frozen peas
4 medium eggs
200ml (7fl oz) coconut cream
1 tsp mild curry paste
1 tbsp sweet chilli sauce
1 tbsp smooth peanut butter
1 large bunch fresh coriander, roughly chopped
mini poppadums and mango chutney to serve

1 Put the rice into a pan with 450ml ($^3/_4$pint) boiling water and cook according to the pack instructions until just tender. Add the frozen peas for the last 5 minutes of cooking time.

2 Meanwhile, put the eggs into a large pan of boiling water and simmer for 6 minutes, then drain and shell.

3 Put the coconut cream, curry paste, chilli sauce and peanut butter into a small pan and whisk together. Heat the sauce gently, stirring, without allowing it to boil.

4 Drain the rice and stir in the chopped coriander and 2 tbsp of the sauce.

5 Divide the rice among four bowls. Cut the eggs into halves and serve on the rice, spooning the remaining coconut sauce over the top. Serve with poppadums and chutney.

Serves 4	EASY		NUTRITIONAL INFORMATION	
	Preparation Time 5 minutes	**Cooking Time** 15 minutes	**Per Serving** 331 calories, 9g fat (of which 12g saturates), 50g carbohydrate, 0.6g salt	Vegetarian Gluten free • Dairy free

Waste Not

Use leftover cooked pasta, beans or potatoes: tip the pasta into a pan of boiling water and bring back to the boil for 30 seconds. Bring the beans or potatoes to room temperature, but there's no need to reboil them.

Pasta with Pesto and Beans

350g (12oz) dried pasta shapes

175g (6oz) fine green beans, roughly chopped

175g (6oz) small salad potatoes, such as Anya, thickly sliced

250g (9oz) fresh pesto sauce

freshly grated Parmesan to serve

1 Bring a large pan of water to the boil. Add the pasta, bring back to the boil and cook for 5 minutes.

2 Add the beans and potatoes to the pan and continue to boil for a further 7–8 minutes until the potatoes are just tender.

3 Drain the pasta, beans and potatoes in a colander, then tip everything back into the pan and stir in the pesto sauce. Serve scattered with freshly grated Parmesan.

EASY		NUTRITIONAL INFORMATION		Serves
Preparation Time 5 minutes	**Cooking Time** 15 minutes	**Per Serving** 738 calories, 38g fat (of which 10g saturates), 74g carbohydrate, 1g salt	Vegetarian	4

Waste Not

- -

Use leftover double cream with a squeeze of lemon juice instead of soured cream.

3 tbsp olive oil

75g (3oz) wholemeal breadcrumbs

1 bunch of spring onions, finely chopped

1 orange pepper, seeded and chopped

1 small green chilli, seeded and finely chopped (see page 33)

1 garlic clove, crushed

1 tsp ground turmeric (optional)

400g can mixed beans, drained

3 tbsp mayonnaise

a small handful of fresh basil, chopped

salt and ground black pepper

soured cream, freshly chopped coriander, lime wedges and tomato salad to serve (optional)

Chilli Bean Cake

1 Heat 2 tbsp olive oil in a non-stick frying pan over a medium heat and fry the breadcrumbs until golden and beginning to crisp. Remove and set aside.

2 Using the same pan, add the remaining oil and fry the spring onions until soft and golden. Add the orange pepper, chilli, garlic and turmeric, if using. Cook, stirring, for 5 minutes.

3 Tip in the beans, mayonnaise, two-thirds of the fried breadcrumbs and the basil. Season with salt and pepper, then mash roughly with a fork. Press the mixture down to flatten. Sprinkle the remaining breadcrumbs over. Fry the bean cake over a medium heat for 4–5 minutes until the base is golden. Remove from the heat, cut into wedges and serve with soured cream, coriander, lime wedges and tomato salad if you like.

Serves 4	EASY		NUTRITIONAL INFORMATION	
	Preparation Time 10 minutes	**Cooking Time** 20 minutes	**Per Serving** 265 calories, 6g fat (of which 1g saturates), 41g carbohydrate, 2.1g salt	Vegetarian Dairy free

Cook's Tip

Make the cheese sauce in the microwave: put the butter, flour and milk into a large microwave-proof bowl and whisk together. Cook in a 900W microwave on full power for 4 minutes, whisking every minute, until the sauce has thickened. Stir in the cheese until it melts. Stir in the mustard and season to taste.

Cheese and Vegetable Bake

250g (9oz) macaroni
1 cauliflower, cut into florets
2 leeks, finely chopped
100g (3¹/₂oz) frozen peas
crusty bread to serve

For the cheese sauce
15g (¹/₂oz) butter
15g (¹/₂oz) plain flour
200ml (7fl oz) skimmed milk
75g (3oz) Parmesan, grated
2 tsp Dijon mustard
25g (1oz) wholemeal breadcrumbs
salt and ground black pepper

1 Cook the macaroni in a large pan of boiling water for 6 minutes, adding the cauliflower and leeks for the last 4 minutes, and the peas for the last 2 minutes.

2 Meanwhile, make the cheese sauce. Melt the butter in a pan and add the flour. Cook for 1–2 minutes, then take off the heat and gradually stir in the milk. Bring to the boil slowly, stirring until the sauce thickens. Stir in 50g (2oz) Parmesan and the mustard. Season with salt and pepper.

3 Preheat the grill to medium. Drain the pasta and the vegetables, and put back in the pan. Add the cheese sauce and mix well. Spoon into a large, shallow 2 litre (3¹/₂ pint) ovenproof dish and scatter the remaining Parmesan and the breadcrumbs over. Grill for 5 minutes or until golden and crisp. Serve hot with bread.

EASY		NUTRITIONAL INFORMATION	Serves
Preparation Time 15 minutes	**Cooking Time** 15 minutes	**Per Serving** 471 calories, 12.9g fat (of which 6.5g saturates), 66.8g carbohydrate, 0.8g salt	4

Mozzarella, Parma Ham and Rocket Pizza

a little plain flour to dust

290g pack pizza base mix

350g (12oz) fresh tomato and chilli pasta sauce

250g (9oz) buffalo mozzarella cheese, drained and roughly chopped

6 slices Parma ham, torn into strips

50g (2oz) rocket

a little extra virgin olive oil to drizzle

salt and ground black pepper

1 Preheat the oven to 200°C (180°C fan oven) mark 6 and lightly flour two large baking sheets. Mix up the pizza base according to the pack instructions. Divide the dough into two and knead each ball on a lightly floured surface for about 5 minutes, then roll them out to make two 23cm (9in) rounds. Put each on to the prepared baking sheet.

2 Divide the tomato sauce between the pizza bases and spread it over, leaving a small border around each edge. Scatter over the mozzarella pieces, then scatter with ham. Season well with salt and pepper.

3 Cook the pizzas for 15–18 minutes until golden. Slide on to a wooden board, top with rocket leaves and drizzle with olive oil. Cut in half to serve.

Cook's Tip

If you're short of time, buy two ready-made pizza bases.

EASY		NUTRITIONAL INFORMATION	Serves
Preparation Time 10 minutes	**Cooking Time** 15–18 minutes	**Per Serving** 508 calories, 19.1g fat (of which 10.5g saturates), 64.2g carbohydrate, 1.9g salt	**4**

Fast Macaroni Cheese

500g (1lb 2oz) macaroni
500ml (18fl oz) crème fraîche
200g (7oz) freshly grated Parmesan
2 tbsp ready-made English or Dijon mustard
5 tbsp freshly chopped flat-leafed parsley
ground black pepper
green salad to serve

1 Bring a large pan of salted water to the boil and cook the macaroni according to the pack instructions. Drain and keep to one side.

2 Preheat the grill to high. Put the crème fraîche into a pan and heat gently. Stir in 175g (6oz) Parmesan, the mustard and parsley and season well with black pepper. Stir the pasta through the sauce, spoon into bowls and sprinkle with the remaining cheese. Grill until golden and serve immediately with salad.

Serves	EASY		NUTRITIONAL INFORMATION
	Preparation Time	**Cooking Time**	**Per Serving**
4	5 minutes	15 minutes	1137 calories, 69.2g fat (of which 44.4g saturates), 96.4g carbohydrate, 2g salt

Mushroom Soufflé Omelette

50g (2oz) small chestnut mushrooms, sliced

3 tbsp crème fraîche

2 medium eggs, separated

15g (½oz) butter

5 fresh chives, roughly chopped

salt and ground black pepper

mixed salad to serve

1 Heat a non-stick frying pan, add the mushrooms and cook, stirring, for 3 minutes to brown slightly, then stir in the crème fraîche and turn off the heat.

2 Lightly beat the egg yolks in a bowl, add 2 tbsp cold water and season with salt and pepper.

3 Put the egg whites into a clean, grease-free bowl and whisk until stiff but not dry, then gently fold into the egg yolks with a large metal spoon. Do not overmix. Heat an 18cm (7in) non-stick frying pan over a medium heat. Add the butter, then the egg mixture, tilting the pan to cover the base. Cook for 3 minutes or until the underside is golden brown.

4 Meanwhile, preheat the grill. Gently reheat the mushrooms and add the chives. Slide the omelette pan under the grill (wrap a wooden handle in foil) for 1 minute or until the surface is just firm and puffy. Tip the mushroom mixture on top. Run a spatula underneath the omelette to loosen it, then carefully fold it and turn out on to a plate. Serve with salad.

EASY		NUTRITIONAL INFORMATION		Serves
Preparation Time 5 minutes	**Cooking Time** 7–10 minutes	**Per Serving** 440 calories, 42g fat (of which 23g saturates), 2g carbohydrate, 0.6g salt	Vegetarian Gluten free	**1**

Cook's Tip

Choose bags or bunches of fresh basil rather than using the leaves of plants sold in pots, as the leaves of herbs in packs or bunches are larger and have a stronger, more peppery flavour.

Aubergine Parmigiana

2 large aubergines, thinly sliced lengthways

2 tbsp olive oil, plus extra to brush

3 fat garlic cloves, thinly sliced

2 x 200ml cartons fresh napoletana sauce

4 ready-roasted red peppers, roughly chopped

20g (³/₄oz) fresh basil, roughly chopped (see Cook's Tip)

150g (5oz) Taleggio or Fontina cheese, coarsely grated

50g (2oz) Parmesan, coarsely grated

salt and ground black pepper

ciabatta to serve

1 Preheat the oven to 200°C (180°C fan oven) mark 6 and preheat the grill to high. Put the aubergines on an oiled baking sheet. Brush with olive oil, scatter over the garlic and season with salt and pepper. Grill for 5–6 minutes until golden.

2 Spread a little napoletana sauce over the base of an oiled ovenproof dish, then cover with a layer of aubergine and peppers, packing the layers together as tightly as you can. Sprinkle a little basil and some of each cheese over the top. Repeat the layers, finishing with a layer of cheese. Season with pepper. Cook in the oven for 20 minutes or until golden. Serve hot with ciabatta.

Serves	EASY		NUTRITIONAL INFORMATION	
4	**Preparation Time** 5 minutes	**Cooking Time** 25 minutes	**Per Serving** 370 calories, 25g fat (of which 11g saturates), 17g carbohydrate, 2.1g salt	Vegetarian

Warm Spicy Chorizo and Chickpea Salad

5 tbsp olive oil

200g (7oz) chorizo or spicy sausage, thinly sliced

225g (8oz) red onion, chopped

1 large red pepper, seeded and roughly chopped

3 garlic cloves, finely chopped

1 tsp cumin seeds

2 x 400g cans chickpeas, drained and rinsed

2 tbsp freshly chopped coriander

juice of 1 lemon

salt and ground black pepper

1 Heat 1 tbsp olive oil in a non-stick frying pan and cook the chorizo or spicy sausage over a medium heat for 1–2 minutes until lightly browned. Remove the chorizo with a slotted spoon and put to one side. Fry the onion in the chorizo oil for 8–10 minutes or until browned.

2 Add the red pepper, garlic, cumin and chickpeas to the onion and cook for a further 5 minutes, stirring frequently to prevent sticking. Remove the pan from the heat and add the chorizo.

3 Add the coriander, lemon juice and remaining olive oil. Season well and serve immediately.

EASY		NUTRITIONAL INFORMATION		Serves
Preparation Time 15 minutes	**Cooking Time** about 15 minutes	**Per Serving** 365 calories, 23.5g fat (of which 5.7g saturates), 27g carbohydrate, 1.3g salt	Dairy free	**6**

Creamy Parma Ham and Artichoke Tagliatelle

500g (1lb 2oz) tagliatelle

500ml (18fl oz) crème fraîche

280g jar roasted artichoke hearts, drained and each cut in half

80g pack Parma ham (6 slices), torn into strips

2 tbsp freshly chopped sage leaves, plus extra to garnish

40g (1½oz) Parmesan shavings

salt and ground black pepper

1 Bring a large pan of water to the boil. Add the pasta, cover and bring back to the boil, then remove the lid and simmer according to the pack instructions.

2 Drain well, reserving a little of the cooking water, then put the pasta back into the pan.

3 Add the crème fraîche to the pan with the artichoke hearts, Parma ham and sage, then stir everything together, thinning the mixture with a ladleful of cooking water. Season well.

4 Spoon into warmed bowls, top with Parmesan shavings and garnish each portion with a sage leaf.

Cook's Tip

Parmesan shavings can be bought in supermarkets. To make your own, use a vegetable peeler to pare off shavings from a block of Parmesan.

Serves	EASY		NUTRITIONAL INFORMATION
4	**Preparation Time** 5 minutes	**Cooking Time** 12 minutes	**Per Serving** 972 calories, 56.3g fat (of which 36.4g saturates), 96.5g carbohydrate, 1.1g salt

Quick and Easy Carbonara

350g (12oz) tagliatelle
150g (5oz) smoked bacon, chopped
1 tbsp olive oil
2 large egg yolks
150ml (¼ pint) double cream
50g (2oz) freshly grated Parmesan
2 tbsp freshly chopped parsley

1 Bring a large pan of water to the boil. Add the pasta, bring back to the boil and cook for 4 minutes or according to the pack instructions.

2 Meanwhile, fry the bacon in the olive oil for 4–5 minutes. Add to the drained pasta and keep hot.

3 Put the egg yolks in a bowl and add the cream. Whisk together. Add to the pasta with the Parmesan and parsley. Toss well and serve.

Serves 4	EASY		NUTRITIONAL INFORMATION
	Preparation Time 5 minutes	**Cooking Time** 10 minutes	**Per Serving** 688 calories, 39g fat (of which 19g saturates), 65g carbohydrate, 1.6g salt

Cook's Tip

Adding the reserved pasta cooking water stops the pasta absorbing too much of the crème fraîche.

Simple Salmon Pasta

500g (1lb 2oz) dried linguine pasta

a little olive oil

1 fat garlic clove, crushed

200ml (7fl oz) half-fat crème fraîche

225g (8oz) hot-smoked salmon, flaked

200g (7oz) peas

two handfuls of basil, roughly torn, to garnish

salt and ground black pepper

1 Cook the pasta in a large pan of boiling salted water according to the pack instructions, then drain, reserving a couple of tablespoons of the cooking water.

2 Meanwhile, heat the olive oil in a large pan, add the garlic and fry gently until golden. Add the crème fraîche, the flaked salmon and peas and stir in. Cook for 1–2 minutes until warmed through, then add the reserved water from the pasta.

3 Toss the pasta into the sauce, season with salt and pepper and serve garnished with the torn basil.

EASY		NUTRITIONAL INFORMATION	Serves
Preparation Time 2 minutes	**Cooking Time** 8 minutes	**Per Serving** 630 calories, 13g fat (of which 5.9g saturates), 100.5g carbohydrate, 2.7g salt	4

3

Meat and Fish in Minutes

Pesto Cod with Butter Beans

4 cod fillets, about 150g (5oz) each

4 tbsp red pepper pesto

2 tbsp olive oil

2 x 400g cans butter beans, drained and rinsed

2 garlic cloves, crushed

225g (8oz) fresh spinach

a squeeze of lemon juice

salt and ground black pepper

1 Preheat the grill to medium. Spread each cod fillet evenly with 1 tbsp red pesto and grill for 10–15 minutes until the flesh is opaque and just cooked.

2 Meanwhile, heat the olive oil in a pan and add the butter beans and garlic. Cook for 10 minutes, stirring occasionally and mashing the beans lightly as they warm through. Season with salt and pepper.

3 About 2–3 minutes before serving, add the spinach to the pan and allow it to wilt. Spoon the butter beans on to four warmed plates and top with the cod and any juices from grilling. Squeeze a little lemon juice over each piece of fish and serve immediately.

Serves 4	EASY		NUTRITIONAL INFORMATION	
	Preparation Time 5 minutes	**Cooking Time** 15 minutes	**Per Serving** 403 calories, 16g fat (of which 3g saturates), 24g carbohydrate, 2.5g salt	Gluten free

4 litres (7 pints) sunflower oil for deep-frying

125g (4oz) self-raising flour

¼ tsp baking powder

¼ tsp salt

1 medium egg

150ml (¼ pint) sparkling mineral water

2 hake fillets, about 125g (4oz) each

450g (1lb) Desirée potatoes, cut into 1cm (½in) chips

salt, vinegar and garlic mayonnaise to serve

Quick Fish and Chips

1 Heat the oil in a deep-fryer to 190°C (test by frying a small cube of bread; it should brown in 20 seconds).

2 Whiz the flour, baking powder, salt, egg and water in a food processor until combined into a batter. Remove the blade from the food processor. Alternatively, put the ingredients in a bowl and beat everything together until smooth. Drop one of the fish fillets into the batter to coat it.

3 Put half the chips in the deep-fryer, then add the battered fish. Fry for 6 minutes or until just cooked, then remove and drain well on kitchen paper. Keep warm if not serving immediately.

4 Drop the remaining fillet into the batter to coat, then repeat step 3 with the remaining chips. Serve with salt, vinegar and garlic mayonnaise.

EASY			NUTRITIONAL INFORMATION		Serves
Preparation Time 15 minutes		**Cooking Time** 12 minutes	**Per Serving** 1186 calories, 79g fat (of which 18g saturates), 73g carbohydrate, 3.2g salt	Dairy free	**2**

Quick Steak Supper

2 sirloin steaks

3 tsp olive oil

4 large mushrooms, sliced

1 red onion, sliced

1 tbsp Dijon mustard

25g (1oz) butter

2 ciabattas, halved lengthways, then quartered, to make
eight pieces

salt and ground black pepper

green salad to serve

1 Heat a griddle or large frying pan until very hot. Rub the steaks with 1 tsp olive oil, season with salt and pepper and fry for about 2 minutes on each side if you like your steak rare, or 4 minutes each side for medium. Remove from the pan and leave to 'rest'.

2 Heat the remaining olive oil in the pan. Add the mushrooms and red onion. Fry, stirring, for 5 minutes or until softened. Stir in the Dijon mustard and butter, and take off the heat.

3 Toast the ciabatta pieces on both sides. Thinly slice the steaks and divide among four pieces of ciabatta. Top with the mushrooms, onion and remaining ciabatta and serve with a green salad.

Try Something Different
- -

Instead of ciabatta, serve the steak with tagliatelle or other pasta.

Serves 4	EASY		NUTRITIONAL INFORMATION
	Preparation Time 10 minutes	**Cooking Time** 10 minutes	**Per Serving** 452 calories, 17g fat (of which 6g saturates), 44g carbohydrate, 1.6g salt

Calf's Liver with Fried Sage and Balsamic Vinegar

15g (½oz) butter plus a little olive oil for frying

12 sage leaves

4 thin slices calf's liver

1–2 tbsp balsamic vinegar

rice, with freshly chopped parsley stirred through, or grilled polenta to serve

1 Melt the butter with a little olive oil in a heavy-based frying pan and when hot add the sage leaves. Cook briefly for 1 minute or so until crisp. Remove, put in a single layer in a shallow dish and keep warm in the oven.

2 Add a little extra oil to the pan, put in two slices of calf's liver and cook quickly for 30 seconds on each side over a high heat. Remove and put on a plate while you quickly cook the remaining two slices.

3 Put all four slices back in the pan, splash the balsamic vinegar over the top and cook for another minute or so. Top with the crispy sage leaves. Serve immediately with rice or polenta.

Serves 4	EASY		NUTRITIONAL INFORMATION	
	Preparation Time 5 minutes	**Cooking Time** 5 minutes	**Per Serving** 88 calories, 6g fat (of which 3g saturates), trace carbohydrate, 0.1g salt	Gluten free

Try Something Different

Use mango instead of the papaya. Make sure it's ripe before you buy it – give it a gentle squeeze to check.
Try the spice rub and fruity relish with pork chops, or with meaty fish such as salmon or tuna steaks.

Cumin-spiced Gammon

a large pinch of ground cumin
a large pinch of paprika
2 tbsp olive oil
2 tsp light muscovado sugar
8 thin smoked gammon steaks, about 125g (4oz) each
2 large ripe papayas
grated zest and juice of 2 limes
½ red chilli, seeded and finely chopped (see page 33)
20g (¾oz) fresh mint, finely chopped
green vegetables to serve

1 Preheat the grill to medium-high. In a small bowl, mix together the cumin, paprika, olive oil and half the sugar. Put the gammon on to a non-stick baking sheet, then brush the spiced oil over each side.

2 Grill the gammon for about 5 minutes on each side, basting once or twice with the juices.

3 Meanwhile, cut each papaya in half, then deseed and peel. Roughly chop half the flesh and put into a bowl. Purée the remaining fruit with the lime juice. Add to the bowl with the lime zest, chilli, mint and remaining sugar. Spoon the mixture on top of the gammon and serve immediately with vegetables.

EASY		NUTRITIONAL INFORMATION		Serves
Preparation Time 10 minutes	**Cooking Time** 10 minutes	**Per Serving** 492 calories, 18g fat (of which 5g saturates), 3g carbohydrate, 13.8g salt	Gluten free Dairy free	**4**

Flash-in-the-pan Pork

700g (1½lb) new potatoes, scrubbed, halved if large
175g (6oz) runner beans, sliced
4 pork escalopes, about 150g (5oz) each
1 tbsp sunflower or olive oil
150ml (¼ pint) hot chicken stock
150ml (¼ pint) apple cider
2 tbsp wholegrain mustard
150g (5oz) Greek yogurt
4 fresh tarragon stems, leaves only
a squeeze of lemon juice
salt and ground black pepper

1 Cook the new potatoes in a large pan of boiling salted water for 10 minutes. Add the beans and cook for a further 5 minutes or until tender. Drain.

2 Meanwhile, season the escalopes with salt and pepper, then heat the oil in a large non-stick frying pan over a medium heat. Cook the pork for 3 minutes on each side or until browned. Remove from the pan and keep warm. Add the stock, cider and mustard to the pan and increase the heat to reduce the liquid by half.

3 Just before serving, reduce the heat and add the yogurt, tarragon leaves and lemon juice. Put the pork back into the pan to coat with the sauce and warm through. Serve with the potatoes and beans.

Serves	EASY		NUTRITIONAL INFORMATION	
4	**Preparation Time** 5 minutes	**Cooking Time** 15 minutes	**Per Serving** 346 calories, 12g fat (of which 4g saturates), 32g carbohydrate, 0.6g salt	Gluten free

Waste Not

Use leftover roast chicken.

Chicken with Spicy Couscous

125g (4oz) couscous

1 ripe mango, peeled, stoned and cut into 2.5cm (1in) chunks

1 tbsp lemon or lime juice

125g tub fresh tomato salsa

3 tbsp mango chutney

3 tbsp orange juice

2 tbsp freshly chopped coriander, plus extra to garnish

200g (7oz) chargrilled chicken fillets, sliced

salt and ground black pepper

lime wedges to garnish

1 Put the couscous in a large bowl and pour 300ml (½ pint) boiling water over. Season well with salt and pepper, then leave to stand for 15 minutes.

2 Put the mango chunks on a plate and sprinkle with the lemon or lime juice.

3 In a small bowl, mix together the tomato salsa, mango chutney, orange juice and coriander.

4 Drain the couscous if necessary, fluff the grains with a fork, then stir in the salsa mixture and check the seasoning. Turn out on to a large serving dish and arrange the chicken and mango on top.

5 Just before serving garnish with lime wedges.

EASY		NUTRITIONAL INFORMATION	Serves
Preparation Time 15 minutes	**Cooking Time** 15 minutes, plus 15 minutes soaking	**Per Serving** 187 calories, 4g fat (of which 1g saturates), 24g carbohydrate, 0.1g salt	**4**

Spiced Chicken with Garlic Butter Beans

4 skinless chicken breasts, about 100g (3½oz) each

1 tbsp olive oil

1 tsp ground coriander

1 tsp ground cumin

100g (3½oz) couscous

3 tbsp extra virgin olive oil

1 garlic clove, sliced

2 x 400g cans butter beans, drained and rinsed

juice of 1 lemon

1 small red onion, thinly sliced

50g (2oz) marinated roasted peppers, drained

2 medium tomatoes, seeded and chopped

1 tbsp freshly chopped coriander

1 tbsp freshly chopped flat-leafed parsley

salt and ground black pepper

1 Put the chicken on a board, cover with clingfilm and flatten lightly with a rolling pin. Put the olive oil into a large bowl with the ground coriander and cumin. Mix together, then add the chicken and turn to coat.

2 Heat a large frying pan and cook the chicken for 5–7 minutes on each side until golden and the juices run clear when pierced with a sharp knife.

3 While the chicken is cooking, put the couscous into a bowl and add 100ml (3½fl oz) boiling water. Cover with clingfilm and set aside.

4 Put the extra virgin olive oil in a small pan with the garlic and butter beans and warm through for 3–4 minutes over a low heat. Stir in the lemon juice and season with salt and pepper.

5 Fluff up the couscous with a fork and tip in the warm butter beans. Add the onion, peppers, tomatoes and herbs and stir together. Slice each chicken breast into four pieces and arrange alongside the bean salad. Serve with a green salad and lemon wedges to squeeze over.

EASY		NUTRITIONAL INFORMATION		Serves
Preparation Time 10 minutes	**Cooking Time** 15 minutes	**Per Serving** 443 calories, 16.1g fat (of which 2.9g saturates), 42.1g carbohydrate, 2g salt	Dairy free	**4**

Cook's Tip

Smoked fish is quite salty so always taste the sauce before seasoning with any extra salt.

Simple Smoked Haddock

25g (1oz) unsalted butter

1 tbsp olive oil

1 garlic clove, thinly sliced

4 thick smoked haddock or cod fillets, about 175g (6oz) each

a small handful of freshly chopped parsley (optional)

finely grated zest of 1 small lemon, plus lemon wedges to serve (optional)

romanesco, cauliflower or broccoli to serve

1 Heat the butter, olive oil and garlic in a large non-stick pan until the mixture starts to foam and sizzle. Put the fish into the pan, skin side down, and fry over a high heat for 10 minutes – this will give a golden crust underneath the fish.

2 Turn the fish over and scatter the parsley, if using, and lemon zest over it, then fry for a further 30 seconds. Put each cooked fillet on to a plate and spoon some of the buttery juices over. Serve with lemon wedges, if using, and steamed romanesco, cauliflower or broccoli.

Serves	EASY		NUTRITIONAL INFORMATION	
4	**Preparation Time** 10 minutes	**Cooking Time** 10 minutes	**Per Serving** 217 calories, 9g fat (of which 4g saturates), 1g carbohydrate, 3.4g salt	Gluten free

Get Ahead

To freeze Complete the recipe, transfer to a freezerproof container, cool, label and freeze for up to three months.
To use Thaw overnight in the fridge. Put in a pan, cover and bring to the boil; reduce the heat to low and simmer until piping hot.

Quick Beef Stroganoff

700g (1½lb) rump or fillet steak, trimmed
50g (2oz) unsalted butter or 4 tbsp olive oil
1 onion, thinly sliced
225g (8oz) brown-cap mushrooms, sliced
3 tbsp brandy
1 tsp French mustard
200ml (7fl oz) crème fraîche
100ml (3½fl oz) double cream
3 tbsp freshly chopped flat-leafed parsley
salt and ground black pepper
rice or noodles to serve

1 Cut the steak into strips about 5mm (¼in) wide and 5cm (2in) long.

2 Heat half the butter or olive oil in a large heavy frying pan over a medium heat. Add the onion and cook gently for 10 minutes or until soft and golden. Remove with a slotted spoon and set aside. Add the mushrooms to the pan and cook, stirring, for 2–3 minutes until golden brown. Remove and set aside.

3 Increase the heat and quickly fry the meat, in two or three batches, for 2–3 minutes, stirring constantly to ensure even browning. Add the brandy and allow it to bubble to reduce.

4 Put the meat, onion and mushrooms back into the pan. Reduce the heat and stir in the mustard, crème fraîche and cream. Heat through, stir in most of the parsley and season with salt and pepper. Serve with rice or noodles, with the remaining parsley scattered over the top.

EASY		NUTRITIONAL INFORMATION		Serves
Preparation Time 10 minutes	**Cooking Time** 20 minutes	**Per Serving** 750 calories, 60g fat (of which 35g saturates), 3g carbohydrate, 0.5g salt	Gluten free	**4**

Italian Sausage Stew

25g (1oz) dried porcini mushrooms

2 tbsp olive oil

1 onion, sliced

2 garlic cloves, chopped

1 small red chilli, seeded and finely chopped (see page 33)

2 fresh rosemary stalks

300g (11oz) whole rustic Italian salami sausages, such as salami Milano, cut into 1cm (½in) slices

400g can chopped tomatoes

200ml (7fl oz) red wine

1 tsp salt

175g (6oz) quick-cook or instant polenta

50g (2oz) butter

50g (2oz) freshly grated Parmesan, plus extra shavings to serve (optional)

75g (3oz) Fontina cheese, cubed

ground black pepper

1 Put the mushrooms in a small bowl, pour over 100ml (3½fl oz) boiling water and soften in the microwave on full power for 3½ minutes, or leave to soak for 20 minutes. Set aside to cool.

2 Heat the olive oil in a large frying pan over a low heat, add the onion, garlic and chilli and cook gently for 5 minutes. Add the leaves from one rosemary stalk to the pan, stirring.

3 Add the salami and fry for 2 minutes on each side or until browned. Drain and chop the soaked mushrooms and add to the pan. Add the tomatoes and wine, then season with pepper. Simmer, uncovered, for 5 minutes.

4 Pour 750ml (1¼ pints) boiling water into a pan and add the salt. Bring back to the boil, pour in the polenta in a steady stream, stirring, and cook according to the pack instructions. Add the butter and both cheeses and mix together well.

5 To serve, divide the polenta among four serving plates and top with the Parmesan shavings, if you like. Spoon some sausage stew alongside each serving of polenta and garnish each with a rosemary sprig. Serve immediately.

Serves 4	EASY		NUTRITIONAL INFORMATION
	Preparation Time 10 minutes, plus soaking	**Cooking Time** 15 minutes	**Per Serving** 443 calories, 35g fat (of which 12g saturates), 6g carbohydrate, 3.4g salt

Try Something Different

Use limes instead of lemons. Knead them on the worktop for 30 seconds before squeezing so they yield as much juice as possible.

Lemon Chicken

4 small skinless chicken breasts, about 125g (4oz) each, cut into chunky strips

juice of 2 lemons

2 tbsp olive oil

4–6 tbsp demerara sugar

salt

green salad to serve

1 Put the chicken strips into a large bowl and season with salt. Add the lemon juice and olive oil and stir to mix.

2 Preheat the grill to medium. Spread the chicken out on a large baking sheet and sprinkle over half the sugar. Grill for 3–4 minutes until caramelised, then turn the chicken over, sprinkle with the remaining sugar and grill until the chicken is cooked through and golden.

3 Divide the chicken among four plates and serve with a green salad.

Serves 4	EASY		NUTRITIONAL INFORMATION	
	Preparation Time 2 minutes	**Cooking Time** 6–8 minutes	**Per Serving** 231 calories, 7g fat (of which 1g saturates), 13g carbohydrate, 0.2g salt	Gluten free Dairy free

Cook's Tips

Make your own mint sauce: finely chop 20g (³/₄oz) fresh mint and mix with 1 tbsp each olive oil and white wine vinegar.

Make your own garlic-infused oil: gently heat 2 tbsp olive oil with peeled, sliced garlic for 5 minutes and use immediately. Do not store.

Lamb Chops with Crispy Garlic Potatoes

2 tbsp mint sauce (see Cook's Tips)

8 small lamb chops

3 medium potatoes, peeled and cut into 5mm (¹/₄in) slices

2 tbsp garlic-infused olive oil (see Cook's Tips)

1 tbsp olive oil

salt and ground black pepper

steamed green beans to serve

1 Spread the mint sauce over the lamb chops and leave to marinate while you prepare the potatoes.

2 Boil the potatoes in a pan of lightly salted water for 2 minutes or until just starting to soften. Drain, tip back into the pan, season with salt and pepper and toss with the garlic oil.

3 Meanwhile, heat the olive oil in a large frying pan and fry the chops for 4–5 minutes on each side until just cooked, adding a splash of boiling water to the pan to make a sauce. Remove the chops and sauce from the pan and keep warm.

4 Add the potatoes to the pan. Fry over a medium heat for 10–12 minutes until crisp and golden. Divide the potatoes, chops and sauce among four plates and serve with green beans.

EASY		NUTRITIONAL INFORMATION		Serves
Preparation Time 10 minutes	**Cooking Time** 20 minutes	**Per Serving** 835 calories, 45g fat (of which 19g saturates), 22g carbohydrate, 0.7g salt	Gluten free Dairy free	4

Cook's Tip

Thai fish sauce is widely used in South-east Asian cooking and is made from fermented anchovies. It adds a salty flavour to food and is called nam pla in Thailand.

Poached Thai Salmon

200g (7oz) Thai jasmine rice

1 tbsp sesame oil

1 red chilli, seeded and finely chopped (see page 33)

5cm (2in) piece fresh root ginger, peeled and finely chopped

1 garlic clove, crushed

1–2 tbsp miso paste (see page 38)

2 tsp Thai fish sauce

4 skinless salmon fillets, about 150g (5oz) each

150g (5oz) fresh shiitake mushrooms, sliced

250g (9oz) pak choi, roughly chopped

100g (3½oz) baby leaf spinach

1 lime, quartered

1 Put the rice into a small pan with 400ml (14fl oz) boiling water. Cover, bring to the boil, then reduce the heat to low. Cook according to the pack instructions.

2 Heat the sesame oil in a large shallow pan or wok, add the chilli, ginger and garlic and cook for 1–2 minutes. Add the miso paste and fish sauce, then pour over 500ml (18fl oz) hot water.

3 Add the salmon and mushrooms, then cover and simmer for 7–8 minutes until fish is just cooked. Steam the pak choi and spinach over boiling water for 4–5 minutes. Serve the salmon with some of the sauce, with the rice, vegetables and lime wedges to squeeze over.

EASY		NUTRITIONAL INFORMATION		Serves
Preparation Time 10 minutes	**Cooking Time** 15 minutes	**Per Serving** 484 calories, 19.1g fat (of which 3.4g saturates), 42.1g carbohydrate, 1.8g salt	Gluten free Dairy free	**4**

50g (2oz) fresh breadcrumbs

a small handful of freshly chopped flat-leafed parsley

2 tbsp capers, chopped

grated zest of 1 lemon

4 haddock or pollack fillets, about 150g (5oz) each

½ tbsp Dijon mustard

juice of ½ lemon

salt and ground black pepper

new potatoes and mixed salad to serve

Crispy Crumbed Fish

1 Preheat the oven to 180°C (160°C fan oven) mark 4. Put the breadcrumbs into a bowl with the parsley, capers and lemon zest. Mix well, then set aside.

2 Put the fish fillets on to a baking tray. Mix the mustard and half the lemon juice in a bowl with a little salt and pepper, then spread over the top of each piece of fish. Spoon the breadcrumb mixture over the top – don't worry if some falls off.

3 Cook in the oven for 10–15 minutes until the fish is cooked and the breadcrumbs are golden. Pour the remaining lemon juice over the top and serve with new potatoes and a mixed salad.

Serves	EASY		NUTRITIONAL INFORMATION	
4	**Preparation Time** 5 minutes	**Cooking Time** 10–15 minutes	**Per Serving** 171 calories, 1g fat (of which trace saturates), 10g carbohydrate, 0.8g salt	Dairy free

Spanish-style Pork

500g (1lb 2oz) pork fillet, trimmed and sliced

2 tbsp olive oil

1 Spanish onion, chopped

2 celery sticks, finely chopped

2 tsp smoked paprika

1 tbsp tomato purée

750ml (1¼ pints) hot chicken stock

400g can butter beans, drained and rinsed

¼ Savoy cabbage, finely shredded

200g (7oz) green beans, trimmed and halved

salt and ground black pepper

1 tbsp freshly chopped rosemary to garnish

lemon wedges and crusty bread to serve

1 Lay the pork out on a board, cover with clingfilm and flatten slightly with a rolling pin. Heat 1 tbsp olive oil in a frying pan and fry the pork over a medium to high heat until browned. Remove from the pan and set aside.

2 Heat the remaining oil and gently fry the onion and celery for 10 minutes or until softened. Stir in the paprika and tomato purée, and cook for 1 minute. Stir in the stock, butter beans and cabbage. Season with salt and pepper.

3 Return the pork to the pan and bring to the boil, then simmer for 10 minutes, adding the green beans for the last 4 minutes. Garnish with rosemary and serve with lemon wedges and crusty bread on the side.

EASY		NUTRITIONAL INFORMATION		Serves
Preparation Time 15 minutes	**Cooking Time** 25 minutes	**Per Serving** 349 calories, 11.9g fat (of which 2.7g saturates), 26.1g carbohydrate, 1.2g salt	Dairy free Gluten free	**4**

4

Cook Once, Eat Twice

Get Ahead

This dish is ideal for freezing for an easy meal another day. Double the quantities and make another meal for four or make two meals for two people and freeze.

Complete the recipe to the end of step 2, then layer the mince and pasta in a freezerproof, heatproof container. Cool and freeze for up to three months.

To use Thaw overnight in the fridge. Bake in the oven at 190°C (170°C fan oven) mark 5 for 25 minutes, then place under a hot grill for 2–3 minutes until bubbling.

Alternatively, make double the meat mixture, freeze half and serve with spaghetti or flour tortillas.

Tagliatelle Bake

1 tbsp olive oil

1 large onion, finely chopped

450g (1lb) minced beef

2 garlic cloves, crushed

290g jar marinated vegetables

2 x 400g cans chopped tomatoes

1 tsp dried marjoram

375g (12oz) fresh garlic and herb tagliatelle

330g jar ready-made cheese sauce

4 tbsp milk

75g (3oz) Cheddar cheese, grated

salt

mixed salad to serve

1 Heat the olive oil in a pan. Add the onion and fry until soft. Add the beef and fry, stirring, until the meat is brown. Add the garlic, marinated vegetables, tomatoes and marjoram. Simmer for 25 minutes or until the meat is tender.

2 Cook the tagliatelle in a pan of boiling salted water according to the pack instructions. Drain, put back into the pan and stir in the cheese sauce and milk. Heat through for 3 minutes.

3 Preheat the grill. Put alternate layers of mince and pasta in a heatproof dish and top with the cheese. Cook under the hot grill until bubbling. Serve with a mixed salad.

Serves 4	EASY		NUTRITIONAL INFORMATION
	Preparation Time 5 minutes	**Cooking Time** 45 minutes	**Per Serving** 935 calories, 42.1g fat (of which 19g saturates), 97.1g carbohydrate, 1.6g salt

Get Ahead

This dish is ideal for freezing for an easy meal another day. Double the quantities and make another meal for four or make two meals for two people and freeze.

Complete the recipe, then transfer to a freezerproof container, cool and freeze for up to three months.

To use Thaw overnight at cool room temperature. Preheat the oven to 180°C (160°C fan oven) mark 4. Bring to the boil on the hob, cover tightly and reheat in the oven for about 30 minutes or until piping hot.

Alternatively, top the cooked beef with a puff pastry lid (see page 103) and bake in a preheated oven at 220°C (200°C fan oven) mark 7 for 30 minutes until the pastry is risen and golden.

Braised Beef

175g (6oz) smoked pancetta or smoked streaky bacon, cut into cubes

2 medium leeks, thickly sliced

1 tbsp olive oil

450g (1lb) braising steak, cut into 5cm (2in) pieces

1 large onion, finely chopped

2 carrots, thickly sliced

2 parsnips, thickly sliced

1 tbsp plain flour

300ml (½ pint) red wine

1–2 tbsp redcurrant jelly

125g (4oz) chestnut mushrooms, halved

freshly chopped flat-leafed parsley to garnish

salt and ground black pepper

mashed potato to serve

1 Preheat the oven to 170°C (150°C fan oven) mark 3. Fry the pancetta or bacon in a shallow flameproof casserole for 2–3 minutes until golden. Add the leeks. Cook for 2 minutes or until the leeks are beginning to colour. Remove with a slotted spoon and set aside.

2 Heat the olive oil in the casserole and fry the beef in batches for 2–3 minutes until golden on all sides. Remove and set aside. Add the onion and fry over a low heat for 5 minutes or until golden. Stir in the carrots and parsnips and fry for 1–2 minutes.

3 Put the beef back into the casserole and stir in the flour to soak up the juices. Gradually add the red wine and 300ml (½ pint) water, then stir in the redcurrant jelly. Season with salt and pepper and bring to the boil. Cover with a tight-fitting lid and cook in the oven for 2 hours.

4 Stir in the leeks, pancetta and mushrooms, re-cover and cook for a further 1 hour. Scatter with parsley and serve with mashed potato.

Serves	EASY		NUTRITIONAL INFORMATION	
4	**Preparation Time** 20 minutes	**Cooking Time** about 3½ hours	**Per Serving** 554 calories, 25.3g fat (of which 8.6g saturates), 33g carbohydrate, 1.7g salt	Dairy free

Get Ahead

This dish is ideal for freezing. Freeze leftover portions separately or double the quantities and freeze half for another day.
Complete the recipe to the end of step 4, then cool and freeze for up to one month.
To use Thaw overnight at cool room temperature. Preheat the oven to 200°C (180°C fan oven) mark 6. Bake for 40–45 minutes until golden and bubbling.

Mushroom and Roasted Potato Bake

900g (2lb) small potatoes, peeled and quartered
6 tbsp olive oil
225g (8oz) onions, roughly chopped
450g (1lb) mixed fresh mushrooms, such as shiitake and brown-cap, roughly chopped
2 garlic cloves, crushed
2 tbsp tomato purée
4 tbsp sun-dried tomato paste
25g (1oz) dried porcini mushrooms, rinsed (optional)
2 tsp freshly chopped thyme
300ml (½ pint) each of dry white wine and vegetable stock
300ml (½ pint) double cream
400g (14oz) large fresh spinach leaves, roughly chopped
175g (6oz) Gruyère cheese
125g (4oz) Parmesan, grated
300ml (½ pint) Greek yogurt
2 medium eggs, beaten
salt and ground black pepper

1 Preheat the oven to 200°C (180°C fan oven) mark 6. Toss the potatoes with 4 tbsp olive oil in a roasting tin and cook for 40 minutes or until tender.

2 Heat the remaining oil in a large heavy-based pan. Add the onions and cook for 10 minutes or until soft, then add the fresh mushrooms and garlic and cook over a high heat for 5 minutes. Stir in the tomato purée and tomato paste, the porcini mushrooms, if using, and the thyme and wine. Bring to the boil and simmer for 2 minutes. Add the stock and cream and bubble for 20 minutes or until well reduced and syrupy. Pour into a 2.4 litre (4¼ pint) ovenproof dish. Stir in the potatoes, spinach, Gruyère and half the Parmesan. Season well with salt and pepper.

3 Combine the yogurt with the eggs and season. Spoon over the vegetable mixture and sprinkle with the remaining Parmesan.

4 Cook in the oven for 30–35 minutes until golden and bubbling. Serve hot.

EASY		NUTRITIONAL INFORMATION		Serves
Preparation Time 15 minutes	**Cooking Time** 1¼ hours	**Per Serving** 809 calories, 62.6g fat (of which 30.6g saturates), 33.1g carbohydrate, 1.7g salt	Gluten free	**6**

Moroccan Chicken with Chickpeas

12 chicken pieces, including thighs, drumsticks and breast

25g (1oz) butter

1 large onion, sliced

2 garlic cloves, crushed

2 tbsp harissa paste

a generous pinch of saffron

1 tsp salt

1 cinnamon stick

600ml (1 pint) chicken stock

75g (3oz) raisins

2 x 400g cans chickpeas, drained and rinsed

ground black pepper

plain naan or pitta bread to serve

1 Heat a large, wide non-stick pan. Add the chicken pieces and fry until well browned all over. Add the butter and, when melted, add the onion and garlic. Cook, stirring, for 5 minutes.

2 Add the harissa, saffron, salt and cinnamon stick, then season well with pepper. Pour in the stock and bring to the boil. Reduce the heat, cover and simmer gently for 25–30 minutes.

3 Add the raisins and chickpeas and bring to the boil. Simmer uncovered for 5–10 minutes.

4 Serve with warm flat bread such as plain naan or pitta.

Get Ahead

This dish is ideal for freezing. Freeze leftover portions separately.

Complete the recipe, then cool quickly. Put in a sealable container and freeze for up to three months.

To use Thaw overnight in the fridge. Put in a pan, cover and bring to the boil. Reduce the heat to low, then reheat for 40 minutes or until the chicken is hot right through.

Instead of bread, serve with couscous or brown rice.

EASY		NUTRITIONAL INFORMATION	Serves
Preparation Time 10 minutes	**Cooking Time** 50 minutes	**Per Serving** 440 calories, 18.1g fat (of which 5.9g saturates), 32.7g carbohydrate, 1g salt	**6**

Get Ahead

This dish is ideal for freezing. Freeze leftover portions separately.

Complete the recipe, then carefully transfer to a freezerproof, heatproof container. Cool and freeze for up to three months.

To use Thaw overnight at cool room temperature. Bake in the oven at 190°C (170°C fan oven) mark 5 for 30 minutes, until bubbling.

Lamb and Leek Hotpot

50g (2oz) butter

400g (14oz) leeks, sliced

1 onion, chopped

800g (1lb 12oz) casserole lamb, cubed

1 tbsp plain flour

1 tbsp olive oil

2 garlic cloves, crushed

800g (1lb 12oz) waxy potatoes such as Desirée, peeled and sliced

3 tbsp freshly chopped parsley

1 tsp freshly chopped thyme

600ml (1 pint) lamb stock

150ml (¼ pint) double cream

salt and ground black pepper

1 Melt half the butter in a 3.5 litre (6¼ pint) flameproof casserole dish over a low heat. Add the leeks and onion, stir to coat, then cover and cook for 10 minutes. Remove and put to one side.

2 Toss the lamb with the flour. Add the olive oil to the casserole and heat, then brown the meat in batches with the garlic and plenty of salt and pepper. Remove and set aside.

3 Preheat the oven to 170°C (150°C fan oven) mark 3. Put half the potatoes in a layer in the casserole and season with salt and pepper. Add the meat, then spoon the leek mixture on top. Arrange a layer of overlapping potatoes on top of that, sprinkle with the parsley and thyme, then pour in the stock.

4 Bring the casserole to the boil, cover, then cook in the oven for about 1 hour 50 minutes. Remove the lid, dot with the remaining butter and add the cream. Cook uncovered for 30–40 minutes until the potatoes are golden brown.

Serves 6	EASY		NUTRITIONAL INFORMATION
	Preparation Time 20 minutes	**Cooking Time** 2 hours 50 minutes	**Per Serving** 549 calories, 37g fat (of which 20g saturates), 25g carbohydrate, 0.5g salt

Get Ahead

This dish is ideal for freezing. Freeze leftover portions separately.

Complete the recipe to the end of step 4. Add the pasta and cook for 10 minutes – it will continue to cook right through when you reheat the Bolognese. Cool, put in a freezerproof container and freeze for up to three months.

To use Thaw overnight at cool room temperature, put in a pan and add 150ml (¼ pint) water. Bring to the boil, then simmer gently for 10 minutes or until the sauce is hot and the pasta is cooked.

Chunky One-pot Bolognese

3 tbsp olive oil

2 large red onions, finely diced

a few fresh rosemary sprigs

1 large aubergine, finely diced

8 plump coarse sausages

350ml (12fl oz) full-bodied red wine

700g (1½lb) passata

4 tbsp sun-dried tomato paste

300ml (½ pint) hot vegetable stock

175g (6oz) small dried pasta, such as orecchiette

salt and ground black pepper

1 Heat 2 tbsp olive oil in a large, shallow non-stick pan. Add the onions and rosemary and cook over a gentle heat for 10 minutes or until soft and golden.

2 Add the aubergine and remaining oil and cook over a medium heat for 8–10 minutes until soft and golden.

3 Meanwhile, pull the skin off the sausages and divide each into four rough chunks. Tip the aubergine mixture on to a plate and add the sausage chunks to the hot pan. You won't need any extra oil.

4 Stir the sausage pieces over a high heat for 6–8 minutes until golden and beginning to turn crisp at the edges. Pour in the wine and allow to bubble for 6–8 minutes until only a little liquid remains. Put the aubergine mixture back into the pan, along with the passata, tomato paste and stock.

5 Stir the pasta into the liquid, cover, then simmer for 20 minutes or until the pasta is cooked. Taste and season with salt and pepper if necessary.

EASY		NUTRITIONAL INFORMATION		Serves
Preparation Time 15 minutes	**Cooking Time** about 1 hour	**Per Serving** 506 calories, 31g fat (of which 11g saturates), 40g carbohydrate, 1.5g salt	Dairy free	**6**

Luxury Smoked Fish Pie

1.1kg (2½lb) Desirée potatoes, peeled and cut into rough chunks

450ml (¾ pint) milk

125g (4oz) butter

125g (4oz) Cheddar cheese, grated

75ml (2½fl oz) dry white wine

150ml (¼ pint) fish stock

450g (1lb) skinless smoked haddock fillet, undyed if possible, cut into wide strips

350g (12oz) skinless salmon fillet, cut into wide strips

40g (1½oz) plain flour

75ml (2½fl oz) double cream

1 tbsp capers, drained, rinsed and chopped

1½ tbsp freshly chopped flat-leafed parsley

2 medium eggs, hard-boiled

salt and ground black pepper

1 Preheat the oven to 180°C (160°C fan oven) mark 4. Put the potatoes into a pan of salted water, bring to the boil, cover and simmer until tender.

2 Warm 100ml (3½fl oz) milk. Drain the potatoes, then put back in the pan over a low heat for 2 minutes. Mash until smooth. Stir in 75g (3oz) butter, half the cheese and the warmed milk; season with salt and pepper. Cover and put to one side.

3 Meanwhile, bring the wine, stock and remaining milk to the boil in a large wide pan. Add the haddock and salmon. Return the liquid to the boil, then reduce the heat to poach the fish gently for 5 minutes or until it flakes easily. Lift the fish with a draining spoon into a 1.4 litre (2½ pint) deep ovenproof dish and flake with a fork if necessary. Put the cooking liquid to one side.

4 Melt the remaining butter in another pan, add the flour and stir until smooth, then cook for 2 minutes. Gradually add the fish liquid, whisking until smooth. Bring to the boil, stirring, and cook for 2 minutes or until thickened. Stir in the cream, capers and parsley, and season with salt and pepper to taste.

5 Shell the eggs and chop roughly. Scatter over the fish then pour the sauce over. Spoon the potato mixture on top and sprinkle with the remaining cheese.

6 Bake the pie for 35–40 minutes until golden and bubbling at the edges. Serve hot.

Get Ahead

Double the ingredient quantities and make two pies, each to serve four people, then freeze one for another day.
Complete the recipe to the end of step 4. Cool the sauce quickly, then complete step 5. Freeze for up to three months.
To use Thaw overnight at cool room temperature. Bake at 190°C (170°C fan oven) mark 5 for 50–60 minutes until golden and bubbling at the edges.

Serves	EASY		NUTRITIONAL INFORMATION
4	**Preparation Time** 30 minutes	**Cooking Time** 1 hour 20 minutes	**Per Serving** 1057 calories, 62.8g fat (of which 33.5g saturates), 66.1g carbohydrate, 3.8g salt

Get Ahead

This dish is ideal for freezing for an easy meal another day. The recipe will make two meals for four people.
Complete the recipe to the end of step 4. Cool quickly, cover and freeze for up to three months.
To use Thaw overnight at cool room temperature. Add 150ml (¼ pint) stock and bring to the boil. Cover and reheat at 180°C (160°C fan oven) mark 4 for 25 minutes; complete the recipe.

Cook's Tip

Marinate the pork for at least 8 hours, or overnight: put it in a large bowl with 6 garlic cloves, 2 tbsp olive oil, 2 tbsp red wine vinegar, 4 tbsp soft brown sugar, a few drops of chilli sauce and 2 tsp each of dried thyme and oregano. Season, mix well, then cover and leave in the fridge.

Winter Hotpot

1.4kg (3lb) boned shoulder of pork, cut into 2.5cm (1in) cubes, marinated (see Cook's Tip)

5 tbsp olive oil

450g (1lb) onions, halved and sliced

2 tbsp tomato purée

2 x 400g cans haricot beans, drained, liquid reserved

2 x 400g cans chopped tomatoes

300ml (½ pint) red wine

4 bay leaves

25g (1oz) butter

125g (4oz) white breadcrumbs from French bread or ciabatta

1 tsp dried oregano

125g (4oz) Gruyère cheese, grated

salt and ground black pepper

fresh thyme sprigs to garnish

1 Drain the pork, putting the marinade to one side. Preheat the oven to 180°C (160°C fan oven) mark 4.

2 Heat 3 tbsp olive oil in a large flameproof casserole and fry the pork in batches until well browned on all sides. Set aside. Add the remaining oil and cook the onions for 10 minutes over a high heat, stirring occasionally, until they are soft and caramelised. Add the tomato purée and cook for 1 minute. Put the meat back into the casserole with the bean liquid, tomatoes, wine, bay leaves and the reserved marinade. Bring to the boil, stirring, then cover and cook in the oven for 2 hours or until the pork is very tender.

3 About 20 minutes before the end of the cooking time, stir in the beans. Increase the oven temperature to 200°C (180°C fan oven) mark 6 and move the pork to a lower shelf. Heat the butter in a roasting tin, add the breadcrumbs and oregano and season. Brown on the top shelf for 10 minutes. Sprinkle the hotpot with the breadcrumbs and grated cheese. Garnish with thyme sprigs and serve.

Serves 8	EASY		NUTRITIONAL INFORMATION
	Preparation Time 20 minutes, plus at least 8 hours marinating	**Cooking Time** 2 hours 20 minutes	**Per Serving** 547 calories, 22.6g fat (of which 8.7g saturates), 30.8g carbohydrate, 1.9g salt

Get Ahead

This dish is ideal for freezing for an easy meal another day. Double the quantities and make another meal for four or make two meals for two people and freeze.
Complete the recipe, cool quickly, then put into a freezerproof container and freeze for up to three months.
To use Thaw overnight at cool room temperature, then put back into a pan. Bring slowly to the boil, then simmer gently for 10–15 minutes until piping hot.

Cook's Tips

If you can't buy prosciutto, thinly cut smoked streaky bacon will work just as well.
Use button mushrooms if you can't find shiitake.

Chicken in Red Wine

8 slices prosciutto

8 large boned and skinned chicken thighs

1 tbsp olive oil

1 fat garlic clove, crushed

about 12 shallots or button onions, peeled

225g (8oz) fresh shiitake mushrooms

1 tbsp plain flour

300ml (½ pint) red wine

300ml (½ pint) hot chicken stock

1 tbsp Worcestershire sauce

1 bay leaf

salt and ground black pepper

crusty bread to serve

1 Wrap a slice of prosciutto around each chicken thigh. Heat the olive oil in a large non-stick frying pan and fry the chicken pieces in batches for 8–10 minutes until golden all over. Transfer to a plate and set aside.

2 Add the garlic and shallots or button onions and fry over a gentle heat for 5 minutes or until the shallots are beginning to soften and turn golden. Stir in the mushrooms and flour and cook over a gentle heat for 1–2 minutes.

3 Put the chicken back in the pan and add the wine, stock, Worcestershire sauce and bay leaf. Season lightly with salt and pepper, bring to the boil for 5 minutes, then cover and simmer over a low heat for 45 minutes or until the chicken is tender. Serve with crusty bread.

EASY		NUTRITIONAL INFORMATION		Serves
Preparation Time 15 minutes	**Cooking Time** 1 hour 10 minutes	**Per Serving** 358 calories, 13.5g fat (of which 3.8g saturates), 8.1g carbohydrate, 1.1g salt	Dairy free	**4**

Steak and Onion Puff Pie

3 tbsp vegetable oil

2 onions, sliced

900g (2lb) casserole beef, cut into chunks

3 tbsp plain flour

500ml (18fl oz) hot beef stock

2 fresh rosemary sprigs, bruised

flour to dust

500g pack puff pastry

1 medium egg, beaten, to glaze

salt and ground black pepper

1 Preheat the oven to 170°C (150°C fan oven) mark 3. Heat 1 tbsp oil in a large flameproof casserole and sauté the onions for 10 minutes or until golden. Lift out and set aside.

2 Sear the meat in the same casserole, in batches, using more oil as necessary, until brown all over. Lift out each batch as soon as it is browned and put to one side.

3 Add the flour to the casserole and cook for 1–2 minutes to brown. Return the onions and beef to the casserole and add the stock and rosemary. Season well with salt and pepper. Cover and bring to the boil, then cook in the oven for $1\frac{1}{2}$ hours or until the meat is tender.

4 About 30 minutes before the end of the cooking time, lightly dust a worksurface with flour and roll out the pastry. Cut out a lid using a 1.1 litre (2 pint) pie dish as a template, or use four 300ml ($\frac{1}{2}$ pint) dishes. Put on a baking sheet and chill.

5 Remove the casserole from the oven, then increase the heat to 220°C (200°C fan oven) mark 7. Pour the casserole into the pie dish (or individual dishes), brush the edge with water and put on the lid. Press down lightly to seal. Lightly score the top and brush over with the egg. Put the dish back on the baking sheet and bake for 30 minutes or until the pastry is risen and golden. Serve immediately.

Get Ahead

Double the ingredient quantities and make two pies, each to serve four people, freezing one for another day.

Complete the recipe to the end of step 3, then cool the casserole quickly. Roll out the pastry as step 4, then put the beef mixture into a pie dish. Brush the dish edge with water, then put on the pastry and press down lightly to seal. Score the pastry. Cover with clingfilm and freeze for up to three months.

To use Thaw overnight at cool room temperature or in the fridge. Lightly score the pastry, brush with beaten egg and cook at 220°C (200°C fan oven) mark 7 for 35 minutes or until the pastry is brown and the filling piping hot.

EASY		NUTRITIONAL INFORMATION	Serves
Preparation Time 30 minutes	**Cooking Time** 2 hours 25 minutes	**Per Serving** 1036 calories, 61.6g fat (of which 9.8g saturates), 64.9g carbohydrate, 1.4g salt	**4**

Get Ahead

- -

This dish is ideal for freezing. Freeze leftover portions separately.

Complete the recipe Cool quickly immediately after adding the beans, then freeze in sealable containers.

To use Thaw overnight in the fridge. Preheat the oven to 170°C (150°C fan oven) mark 3. Put in a flameproof casserole, cover and bring to the boil on the hob. Transfer to the oven and cook for 45 minutes.

Braised Lamb Shanks with Cannellini Beans

3 tbsp olive oil

6 lamb shanks

1 large onion, chopped

3 carrots, sliced

3 celery sticks, sliced

2 garlic cloves, crushed

2 x 400g cans chopped tomatoes

150ml (¼ pint) balsamic vinegar

2 bay leaves

2 x 400g cans cannellini beans, drained and rinsed

salt and ground black pepper

crusty bread to serve

1 Preheat the oven to 170°C (150°C fan oven) mark 3. Heat the olive oil in a large flameproof casserole. Add the lamb shanks in batches and brown all over. Remove from the pan and set aside.

2 Add the onion, carrots, celery and garlic to the pan and cook gently until beginning to colour. Return the lamb to the pan. Add the tomatoes and balsamic vinegar to the pan, stirring well. Season with salt and pepper and add the bay leaves. Bring to the boil, cover and cook for 5 minutes on the hob, then transfer to the oven for 1½–2 hours or until the shanks are nearly tender.

3 Remove the dish from the oven and add the beans. Cover and put back in the oven for a further 30 minutes. Serve with crusty bread.

Serves	EASY		NUTRITIONAL INFORMATION	
6	**Preparation Time** 15 minutes	**Cooking Time** 3 hours	**Per Serving** 434 calories, 21.6g fat (of which 8g saturates), 26.8g carbohydrate, 1.6g salt	Gluten free Dairy free

Cook's Tip

Use leftover roast chicken in salads and stir-fries, soups and curries. Use the stripped carcass to make chicken stock.

Perfect Roast Chicken

1.8kg (4lb) chicken
25g (1oz) butter, softened
2 tbsp olive oil
1 lemon, cut in half
1 small head of garlic, cut in half horizontally
salt and ground black pepper
roast potatoes and vegetables to serve

1 Preheat the oven to 220°C (200°C fan oven) mark 7. Put the chicken in a roasting tin just large enough to hold it comfortably. Spread the butter all over the chicken, then drizzle with the olive oil and season with salt and pepper.

2 Squeeze the lemon juice over it, then put one lemon half inside the chicken. Put the other half and the garlic into the roasting tin.

3 Put the chicken into the oven for 15 minutes, then turn the heat down to 190°C (170°C fan oven) mark 5 and cook for a further 45 minutes–1 hour until the leg juices run clear when pierced with a skewer. Baste from time to time with the pan juices. Add a splash of water to the tin if the juices dry out.

4 Put the chicken on a warm plate, cover with foil and 'rest' for 10 minutes, so the juices settle back into the meat, making it moist and easier to slice. Mash some of the garlic into the pan juices and serve the gravy with the chicken, with potatoes and vegetables.

EASY		NUTRITIONAL INFORMATION		Serves
Preparation Time 5 minutes	**Cooking Time** 1 hour–1¼ hours, plus resting	**Per Serving** 639 calories, 46g fat (of which 13g saturates), 0g carbohydrate, 0.6g salt	Gluten free	**4**

Italian Lamb

2 half-leg knuckles of lamb

2 tbsp olive oil

75g (3oz) butter

275g (10oz) onions, finely chopped

175g (6oz) carrots, finely chopped

175g (6oz) celery, finely chopped

2 tbsp dried porcini pieces or 125g (4oz) finely chopped brown-cap mushrooms

9 pieces sun-dried tomato, finely chopped

150g (5oz) Italian spicy sausage or salami, thickly sliced

600ml (1 pint) red wine

400g (14oz) passata

600ml (1 pint) vegetable stock

125g (4oz) dried pasta shapes

15g (½oz) freshly grated Parmesan

fresh flat-leafed parsley sprigs to garnish

Get Ahead

This dish is ideal for freezing. Freeze leftover portions separately.

Complete the recipe to the end of step 4. Cool quickly, then freeze for up to three months.

To use Thaw overnight at cool room temperature. Put in a flameproof casserole, cover and bring to the boil on the hob. Complete the recipe from step 6.

1 Preheat the oven to 240°C (220°C fan oven) mark 9. Put the lamb in a large roasting tin and drizzle 1 tbsp olive oi over it. Roast for 35 minutes.

2 Meanwhile, melt the butter with the remaining oil in a large flameproof casserole. Stir in the onions, carrots and celery and cook, stirring, for 10–15 minutes until golden and soft. Stir in the porcini pieces or mushrooms and cook for a further 2–3 minutes.

3 Add the sun-dried tomatoes, sausage, wine, passata and stock to the pan, then bring to the boil and simmer for 10 minutes.

4 Lift the lamb from the roasting tin, add to the tomato sauce and cover with a tight-fitting lid. Reduce the temperature to 170°C (150°C fan oven) mark 3 and cook for a further 3 hours or until the lamb is falling off the bone.

5 Lift the lamb from the casserole on to a deep, heatproof serving dish. Cover loosely with foil and keep warm in a low oven.

6 Put the casserole on the hob, stir in the pasta and bring back to the boil. Simmer for 10 minutes or until the pasta is tender. Stir in the Parmesan just before serving.

7 Carve the lamb into large pieces and serve with the pasta sauce, garnished with parsley.

Serves 4	A LITTLE EFFORT		NUTRITIONAL INFORMATION
	Preparation Time 35 minutes	**Cooking Time** 3¾ hours	**Per Serving** 785 calories, 52.3g fat (of which 17.6g saturates), 20.1g carbohydrate, 3.2g salt

5

Speedy Puddings

Quick Lemon Mousse

6 tbsp lemon curd

300ml (½ pint) double cream, whipped

fresh blueberries to decorate

1 Gently stir the lemon curd through the double cream until combined, and decorate with blueberries.

Serves 4	EASY		NUTRITIONAL INFORMATION	
	Preparation Time 1–2 minutes		**Per Serving** 334 calories, 30g fat (of which 18g saturates), 16g carbohydrate, 0.1g salt	Vegetarian Gluten free

Try Something Different

Replace the brandy with Grand Marnier and use orange-flavoured plain chocolate.

Chocolate Crêpes with a Boozy Sauce

100g (3½oz) plain flour, sifted

a pinch of salt

1 medium egg

300ml (½ pint) milk

sunflower oil for frying

50g (2oz) plain chocolate (at least 70 per cent cocoa solids), roughly chopped

100g (3½oz) unsalted butter

100g (3½oz) light muscovado sugar, plus extra to sprinkle

4 tbsp brandy

1 Put the flour and salt in a bowl, make a well in the centre and add the egg. Use a balloon whisk to mix the egg with a little of the flour, then gradually add the milk to make a smooth batter. Cover and leave to stand for about 20 minutes.

2 Pour the batter into a jug. Heat 1 tsp oil in a 23cm (9in) frying pan, then pour in 100ml (3½fl oz) batter, tilting the pan so that the mixture coats the bottom, and fry for 1–2 minutes until golden underneath. Turn carefully and fry the other side. Tip on to a plate, cover with greaseproof paper and repeat with the remaining batter, using more oil as needed.

3 Divide the chocolate among the crêpes. Fold each crêpe in half, and then in half again.

4 Put the butter and sugar in a heavy-based frying pan over a low heat. Add the brandy and stir. Slide the crêpes into the pan and cook for 3–4 minutes to melt the chocolate. Serve drizzled with sauce and sprinkled with sugar.

EASY		NUTRITIONAL INFORMATION		Serves
Preparation Time 5 minutes, plus 20 minutes standing	**Cooking Time** 20 minutes	**Per Serving** 594 calories, 35g fat (of which 17g saturates), 35g carbohydrate, 0.5g salt	Vegetarian	**4**

Pear and Blackberry Crumble

450g (1lb) pears, peeled, cored and chopped, tossed with the juice of 1 lemon

225g (8oz) golden caster sugar

1 tsp mixed spice

450g (1lb) blackberries

cream, custard or ice cream to serve

For the crumble topping

100g (3½oz) butter, chopped, plus extra to grease

225g (8oz) plain flour

75g (3oz) ground almonds

1 Put the pears and lemon juice in a bowl, add 100g (3½oz) sugar and the mixed spice, then add the blackberries and toss thoroughly to coat.

2 Preheat the oven to 200°C (180°C fan oven) mark 6. Lightly butter a 1.8 litre (3¼ pint) shallow ovenproof dish, then carefully tip the fruit into the dish in an even layer.

3 Put the butter, flour, ground almonds and the remaining sugar in a food processor and pulse until the mixture begins to resemble breadcrumbs. Tip into a bowl. (Alternatively, rub the butter into the flour in a large bowl by hand or using a pastry cutter. Stir in the ground almonds and the remaining sugar.) Bring parts of the mixture together with your hands to make lumps.

4 Spoon the crumble topping evenly over the fruit, then bake for 35–45 minutes until the fruit is tender and the crumble is golden and bubbling. Serve with cream, custard or ice cream.

Cook's Tip

A versatile recipe which can be popped in the oven while you whip up your main course.
Make double the amount of crumble topping and freeze half for an easy pudding another day.
Crumble is a great way to use leftover, slightly overripe fruit. Replace the pears with apples, or omit the blackberries and use 700g (1½lb) plums or rhubarb instead. You could also use gooseberries (omit the spice), or try 450g (1lb) rhubarb with 450g (1lb) strawberries.

Serves 6	EASY		NUTRITIONAL INFORMATION	
	Preparation Time 20 minutes	**Cooking Time** 35–45 minutes	**Per Serving** 525 calories, 21g fat (of which 9g saturates), 81g carbohydrate, 0.3g salt	Vegetarian

Try Something Different

Use raspberries or blueberries instead of the strawberries.

Strawberry Brûlée

250g (9oz) strawberries, hulled and sliced

2 tsp golden icing sugar

1 vanilla pod

400g (14oz) Greek yogurt

100g (3½oz) golden caster sugar

1 Divide the strawberries among four ramekins and sprinkle with icing sugar.

2 Scrape the seeds from the vanilla pod and stir into the yogurt, then spread the mixture evenly over the fruit.

3 Preheat the grill to high. Sprinkle the caster sugar evenly over the yogurt until it's well covered.

4 Put the ramekins on a baking sheet or into the grill pan and grill until the sugar turns dark brown and caramelises. Leave for 15 minutes or until the caramel is cool enough to eat, or chill for up to 2 hours before serving.

Serves 4	EASY		NUTRITIONAL INFORMATION	
	Preparation Time 15 minutes, plus chilling	**Cooking Time** 5 minutes	**Per Serving** 240 calories, 10g fat (of which 5g saturates), 35g carbohydrate, 0.2g salt	Vegetarian Gluten free

Cook's Tip

To freeze bananas, peel and slice them thinly, then put the slices on a large non-stick baking tray and put into the freezer for 1 hour or until frozen. Transfer to a plastic bag and store in the freezer until needed.

Slightly over-ripe bananas are ideal for this recipe.

Instant Banana Ice Cream

6 ripe bananas, about 700g (1½lb), peeled, cut into thin slices and frozen (see Cook's Tip)

1–2 tbsp virtually fat-free fromage frais

1–2 tbsp orange juice

1 tsp vanilla extract

a splash of rum or Cointreau (optional)

a few drops of lime juice to taste

1 Leave the frozen bananas to stand at room temperature for 2–3 minutes. Put the still-frozen pieces in a food processor or blender with 1 tbsp fromage frais, 1 tbsp orange juice, the vanilla extract and the rum or liqueur, if you like.

2 Whiz until smooth, scraping down the sides of the bowl and adding more fromage frais and orange juice as necessary to give a creamy consistency. Add lime juice to taste and serve at once or tip into a freezer container and freeze for up to one month.

EASY	NUTRITIONAL INFORMATION		Serves
Preparation Time 5 minutes, plus about 1 hour freezing	**Per Serving** 171 calories, 0.5g fat (of which 0.2g saturates), 41.3g carbohydrate, 0g salt	Vegetarian Gluten free	**4**

Express Apple Tart

375g pack ready-rolled puff pastry

500g (1lb 2oz) dessert apples, such as Cox's, cored and thinly sliced, then tossed in the juice of 1 lemon

golden icing sugar to dust

1 Preheat the oven to 200°C (180°C fan oven) mark 6. Put the pastry on to a 28 x 38cm (11 x 15in) baking sheet and lightly roll over it with a rolling pin to smooth down the pastry. Score lightly around the edge, leaving a 3cm (1¼in) border.

2 Put the apple slices on top of the pastry within the border. Turn the edge of the pastry halfway over to reach the edge of the apples, press down and use your fingers to crimp the edge.

3 Dust heavily with icing sugar. Bake for 20 minutes or until the pastry is cooked and the sugar has caramelised. Serve warm, dusted with more icing sugar.

EASY		NUTRITIONAL INFORMATION		Serves
Preparation Time 10 minutes	**Cooking Time** 20 minutes	**Per Serving** 197 calories, 11.6g fat (of which 0g saturates), 22.9g carbohydrate, 0.4g salt	Vegetarian	**8**

Try Something Different

Caribbean Crush: replace the sugar and liqueur with dulce de leche toffee sauce and the strawberries with sliced bananas.

Eton Mess

200g (7oz) fromage frais, chilled
200g (7oz) low-fat Greek yogurt, chilled
1 tbsp golden caster sugar
2 tbsp strawberry liqueur
6 meringues, roughly crushed
350g (12oz) strawberries, hulled and halved

1 Put the fromage frais and yogurt into a large bowl and stir to combine.

2 Add the sugar, strawberry liqueur, meringues and strawberries. Mix together gently and divide among six serving dishes.

Serves	EASY		NUTRITIONAL INFORMATION	
6	**Preparation Time** 10 minutes		**Per Serving** 198 calories, 5g fat (of which 3g saturates), 33g carbohydrate, 0.1g salt	Vegetarian Gluten free

Cook's Tip

Quark is a smooth soft white cheese, with a texture between yogurt and fromage frais. Fromage frais can be used instead.

250ml (9fl oz) cold coffee

2 tbsp coffee liqueur, such as Kahlúa or Tia Maria

24 sponge fingers

2 medium eggs, separated

3 tbsp icing sugar

500g (1lb 2oz) quark (see Cook's Tip)

1 tsp vanilla extract

cocoa powder to dust

Tiramisù

1 Pour the cold coffee and coffee liqueur into a bowl. Dip 12 of the sponge fingers into the liquid, and put into six serving dishes or one large dish.

2 Put the egg whites into a clean, grease-free bowl and whisk until they form soft peaks. In a separate bowl, whisk together the egg yolks, icing sugar, quark and vanilla. Fold in the whites.

3 Spoon half the quark mixture over the sponges. Dip the remaining sponge fingers in the coffee mixture, then put on top. Cover with the remaining quark mixture. Dust with cocoa powder and serve.

EASY	NUTRITIONAL INFORMATION		Serves
Preparation Time 20 minutes	**Per Serving** 344 calories, 16g fat (of which 4g saturates), 39g carbohydrate, 0.5g salt	Vegetarian	**6**

Fruity Fool

500g carton summer fruit compote

500g carton fresh custard

1 Divide half the compote among six serving glasses, then add a thin layer of custard. Repeat the process until all the compote and custard have been used.

2 Stir each fool once to swirl the custard and compote together, then serve.

Serves 6	EASY		NUTRITIONAL INFORMATION		
	Preparation Time 1–2 minutes		**Per Serving** 159 calories, 2g fat (of which trace saturates), 31g carbohydrate, 0.1g salt		Vegetarian Gluten free

Cook's Tip

Slightly over-ripe bananas are ideal for this recipe.

Sticky Banoffee Pies

150g (5oz) digestive biscuits
75g (3oz) unsalted butter, melted, plus extra to grease
1 tsp ground ginger (optional)
450g (1lb) dulce de leche toffee sauce
4 bananas, peeled, sliced and tossed in the juice of 1 lemon
300ml (½ pint) double cream, lightly whipped
plain chocolate shavings

1 Put the biscuits in a food processor and whiz until they resemble fine crumbs. (Alternatively, put them in a plastic bag and crush with a rolling pin. Transfer to a bowl.) Add the melted butter and ginger, if using, then process, or stir well, for 1 minute to combine.

2 Butter six 10cm (4in) rings or tartlet tins and line with greaseproof paper. Press the biscuit mixture into each ring. Divide the toffee sauce equally among the rings and top with the bananas. Pipe or spoon on the cream, sprinkle with chocolate shavings and chill. Remove from the rings or tins to serve.

EASY		**NUTRITIONAL INFORMATION**		**Serves**
Preparation Time 15 minutes, plus chilling		**Per Serving** 827 calories, 55g fat (of which 32g saturates), 84g carbohydrate, 1.2g salt	Vegetarian	**6**

Microwave Sticky Toffee Puddings

75g (3oz) mixed dried fruit
75g (3oz) pitted dates, roughly chopped
¾ tsp bicarbonate of soda
150g (5oz) light muscovado sugar
75g (3oz) butter, softened, plus extra to grease
2 medium eggs, beaten
½ tsp vanilla extract
175g (6oz) self-raising flour

For the toffee sauce

125g (4oz) butter
175g (6oz) light muscovado sugar
4 tbsp double cream
25g (1oz) pecan nuts, roughly chopped

1 Grease and baseline six 250ml (9fl oz) cups. Put the dried fruit and bicarbonate of soda in a bowl and pour over 175ml (6fl oz) boiling water. Set side.

2 In a separate bowl, beat the sugar and butter for 1–2 minutes until light and fluffy. Beat in the eggs and vanilla extract, then sift over the flour and fold it into the fruit mixture.

3 Spoon into the cups. Cover very loosely with microwave film and cook three cups on Medium or 600W for 6 minutes in the microwave. Remove the microwave film from the puddings and leave to stand for 1 minute. Repeat with the remaining cups.

4 To make the sauce, put the butter, sugar and cream in a pan and heat gently, stirring well. Pour the sauce over the puddings and sprinkle on the chopped nuts.

Cook's Tip

The puddings can also be baked in a conventional oven, although this takes a little longer. Preheat the oven to 200°C (180°C fan oven) mark 6. Spoon the mixture into buttered heatproof cups, cover with foil, and put on to a baking sheet. Bake for 30 minutes or until soft and springy and a skewer comes out clean.

Serves 6	EASY		NUTRITIONAL INFORMATION	
	Preparation Time 15 minutes	**Cooking Time** 12 minutes	**Per Serving** 720 calories, 37.7g fat (of which 21.7g saturates), 96.2g carbohydrate, 1g salt	Vegetarian

Quick Chocolate Slices

225g (8oz) butter or olive oil spread
3 tbsp golden syrup
50g (2oz) cocoa, sifted
300g pack digestive biscuits, crushed
400g (14oz) plain chocolate (at least 70 per cent cocoa solids), broken into pieces

1 Put the butter or olive oil spread in a bowl and add the golden syrup and cocoa. Melt in a 900W microwave on High for 20 seconds, or until melted. Alternatively, melt in a pan over a very low heat. Mix everything together.

2 Remove from the heat and stir in the biscuits. Mix well until thoroughly coated in chocolate, crushing down any large pieces of biscuit.

3 Turn into a greased 25.5 x 16.5cm (10 x 6½in) rectangular tin. Cool, cover and chill for 20 minutes.

4 Melt the chocolate in a heatproof bowl in a 900W microwave on High for 1 minute 40 seconds, stirring twice. Alternatively melt over a pan of gently simmering water. Stir once more and pour over the chocolate biscuit base, then chill for 20 minutes. Cut in half lengthways and cut each half into 20 rectangular fingers.

Makes 40	EASY		NUTRITIONAL INFORMATION	
	Preparation Time 10 minutes	**Cooking Time** 2 minutes	**Per Slice** 137 calories, 9.3g fat (of which 5.5g saturates), 12.7g carbohydrate, 0.3g salt	Vegetarian

Try Something Different

Serve the mixture warm as a sauce for vanilla ice cream.

Cheat's Chocolate Pots

500g carton fresh custard

200g (7oz) plain chocolate (at least 50 per cent cocoa solids), broken into pieces

1 Put the custard in a small pan with the chocolate pieces. Heat gently, stirring all the time, until the chocolate has melted.

2 Pour the mixture into four small coffee cups and chill in the fridge for 30 minutes to 1 hour before serving.

EASY		NUTRITIONAL INFORMATION		Serves
Preparation Time 5 minutes, plus chilling	**Cooking Time** 5 minutes	**Per Serving** 385 calories, 16.9g fat (of which 8.5g saturates), 52.8g carbohydrate, 0.1g salt	Vegetarian	4

Index

COOKING MEASURES

TEMPERATURE

°C	Fan oven	Gas mark	°C	Fan oven	Gas mark
110	90	¼	190	170	5
130	110	½	200	180	6
140	120	1	220	200	7
150	130	2	230	210	8
170	150	3	240	220	9
180	160	4			

LIQUIDS

Metric	Imperial	Metric	Imperial
5ml	1 tsp	200ml	7fl oz
15ml	1 tbsp	250ml	9fl oz
25ml	1fl oz	300ml	½ pint
50ml	2fl oz	500ml	18fl oz
100ml	3½fl oz	600ml	1 pint
125ml	4fl oz	900ml	1½ pints
150ml	5fl oz / ¼ pint	1 litre	1¾ pints
175ml	6fl oz		

MEASURES

Metric	Imperial	Metric	Imperial
5mm	¼in	10cm	4in
1cm	½in	15cm	6in
2cm	¾in	18cm	7in
2.5cm	1in	20.5cm	8in
3cm	1¼in	23cm	9in
4cm	1½in	25.5cm	10in
5cm	2in	28cm	11in
7.5cm	3in	30.5cm	12in

WEIGHTS

Metric	Imperial	Metric	Imperial
15g	½oz	275g	10oz
25g	1oz	300g	11oz
40g	1½oz	350g	12oz
50g	2oz	375g	13oz
75g	3oz	400g	14oz
100g	3½oz	425g	15oz
125g	4oz	450g	1lb
150g	5oz	550g	1¼lb
175g	6oz	700g	1½lb
200g	7oz	900g	2lb
225g	8oz	1.1kg	2½lb
250g	9oz		

Always remember...

- Ovens and grills must be preheated to the specified temperature.
- For fan ovens the temperature should be set to 20°C less.
- Use one set of measurements; do not mix metric and imperial.
- All spoon measures are level.

NOTES

- Both metric and imperial measures are given for the recipes. Follow either set of measures, not a mixture of both, as they are not interchangeable.
- All spoon measures are level. 1 tsp = 5ml spoon; 1 tbsp = 15ml spoon.
- Ovens and grills must be preheated to the specified temperature.
- Use sea salt and freshly ground black pepper unless otherwise suggested.
- Fresh herbs should be used unless dried herbs are specified in a recipe.
- Medium eggs should be used except where otherwise specified. Free-range eggs are recommended.
- Note that certain recipes, including mayonnaise and some cold desserts, contain raw or lightly cooked eggs. The young, elderly, pregnant women and anyone with an immune-deficiency disease should avoid these, because of the slight risk of salmonella.
- Calorie, fat, salt and carbohydrate counts per serving are provided for the recipes.
- If you are following a gluten- or dairy-free diet, check the labels on all pre-packaged food goods.
- Nutritional information for serving suggestions do not take gluten- or dairy-free diets into account.

Picture credits
Photographers: Craig Robertson (Basics photography and pages 32, 38, 39, 40, 45, 51, 54, 59, 60, 68, 69, 71, 74, 75, 79, 81, 86, 96, 100, 110, 111, 113, 115, 118, 119, 120); Nicki Dowey (pages 34, 35, 47, 52, 53, 64, 72, 73, 78, 114, 121, 126); Neil Barclay (pages 36, 41, 42, 44, 46, 55, 58, 61, 63, 65, 76, 84, 87, 91, 94, 97, 99, 101, 102, 104, 107, 116, 123, 124, 125); Lucinda Symons (pages 14, 16, 33, 56, 92, 93, 105)